HOW TO SPARK A MARRIAGE WHEN THE KIDS LEAVE HOME

PREVIOUS BOOKS BY THE AUTHOR

PATHWAYS TO PERSONAL CONTENTMENT (Prentice-Hall)
POWER TO GET WHAT YOU WANT OUT OF LIFE (Prentice-Hall)
SHADOWS IN THE VALLEY (Doubleday)

HOW TO SPARK A MARRIAGE WHEN THE KIDS LEAVE HOME

FRANK A. KOSTYU

EPWORTH METHODIST CHURCH
HOPE VALLEY ROAD
DURHAM, NORTH CAROLINA

A PILGRIM PRESS BOOK
PHILADELPHIA

Copyright © 1972 United Church Press
Library of Congress Catalog Card Number 72-075098
ISBN 0–8298–0231–2

TO MARJORIE

**WHO HELPED WRITE THIS BOOK
BY LIVING WITH ME ALL THESE YEARS**

CONTENTS

PREFACE 9

1 WHY GOOD MARRIAGES TEND TO BE FRAGILE 11
Times Have Changed/Overly High Expectations/Women's Liberation/Candlelight and Romance/The Vice of Advice/"Keeping Up with the Joneses"/Crossing the Finish Line/The Problems of Sex/Conclusion

2 THE GRASS LOOKS GREENER 25
The Scope of the Problem/New Concepts but Still the Tradition/Physical Characteristics of Middle Age/Adjusting to the Problem

3 KEEP THE LINES OPEN 37
Transmission Lines/Listen/Tell It like It Is/Accessibility/Something to Steer by

4 KEEP YOUR MARRIAGE ROLLING 53
Mid-marriage Slowdown/The Green-eyed Monster/Personality Changes/Sexual Relations Cool/Boredom vs. Vim and Vigor/What Can You Do?

5 COPING WITH A CRISIS 66
Unemployment as a Marriage Factor/Finances/Miles Apart/In Sickness and in Health/Dear Mom and Dad/Tarrying Long at the Wine/Separation by Death/Doubtful Advice/Fate in the Stars?/A Good Friend Is Not So Good/The Encounter Groups/Where Can You Turn?/Steps for Handling Problems

6 LET'S QUARREL CONSTRUCTIVELY 83
The Danger of Unexpressed Anger/Anger Is an Alarm System/Watch Out!/Guidelines to a Healthy Quarrel/The End of the Argument

7 SEX IS BEAUTIFUL—AND ENJOYABLE 93
More than Automated Machines/"There's Snow on the Roof, but the Fire Still Burns"/Problems Are Not Insurmountable/Too Much or Not Enough?/A Game to Play

8 KEEP THE JOYOUS OUTLOOK 111
What Is Humor?/Developing a Sense of Humor/Outlook Is All-important/Thoughts to Remember

TEST YOURSELF 123

BIBLIOGRAPHY 126

"Wake up, Harold! It's 1971 and the children are grown and gone."

Drawing by Henry Martin; copyright 1970 Saturday Review, Inc.

PREFACE

The cartoon in the *Saturday Review* points up one of our most pressing problems today: how to handle a marriage when the children have left home. Too many of us are unprepared for such a situation. We suddenly realize that our family has gone and that we are faced with a new year, a new form of living.

Unprepared, we wallow in the problem. As often happens, this is the time in a marriage that becomes most dangerous so far as divorce or separation is concerned. Man and wife are left alone, rattling around in a house that is suddenly too big. They may realize that they have not had much time for each other in the past. Perhaps the situation has become so serious that the only conclusion agreed upon is separation. Husband and wife may have previously suspected that they no longer love each other as they did in courtship and early marriage but have avoided the confrontation while their children were at home. Now they are at a loss as to what to do. Other couples still love each other but feel they have somehow drifted apart through the years. Once their children have left, they are confused and unhappy, not knowing how to proceed.

Let me hasten to add that families are not necessarily going to break up when the children are no longer there. To some, the time is traumatic and could jeopardize a good relationship. Patience and understanding can alleviate the situation. To others, the time is a beginning of a whole new kind of life and love, more fulfilling and satisfying than before.

This book was written to illustrate some ways of handling the problems that arise when we suddenly realize the children are gone and we genuinely want to strengthen our marriage relationship. Advance preparation can help. One couple, with tongue in cheek, commented that they did not have to face such a problem. "We planned for such an eventuality," said the wife. "We had one child early in our marriage and another fifteen years later. By the time the second one left home, we were too doddering to be separated." This solution, if such it can be called, usually occurs only by accident rather than by good planning and cannot be relied upon. We need to establish a firm ground so that the rest of our lives together will be vital and satisfying.

The material for this book grew out of information gathered throughout a twenty-year pastorate during which many types of problems involving marriage were brought to my attention. Some I was able to cope with; others I passed along to those trained far more extensively in such matters than I. Another qualification I have for writing this book is the fact that I speak from experience, both of my friends and of my own. Marjorie and I have been married for twenty-seven years and have three children who have left or are in the process of leaving home: Joel, who is now married; Paul, who is in college; and Kathy, who will be leaving for college by the time these words find their way into print.

Because people differ and marriage relationships are not alike, some parts of the book are more applicable than others to certain situations. I do not present a foolproof formula for a guaranteed happy marriage but rather, I hope, thought-provoking illustrations and ideas which can help you if you apply them to your personal lives. A happy marriage does not just happen; its partners must make the needed effort. The rewards of such a life together are so enjoyable, however, that the effort is indeed worthwhile.

Each chapter, in addition to pointing out the perplexities which can arise, will contain illustrations with which the reader can identify. Flexible suggestions are interspersed, and at the end of the chapters are helpful rules and exercises to follow.

Frank A. Kostyu
Montclair, New Jersey

1 WHY GOOD MARRIAGES TEND TO BE FRAGILE

June Haver MacMurray, wife of one of television's most popular stars, Fred MacMurray, said in observing marriages of people she knows that the happiest couples are those who do not need a constant stream of people close to them. She recalled that a friend of hers said, "I've got it made. So long as I have hot canapes on the bar, a pitcher of cold martinis, and a swinging party in the making, my husband will love me forever." Six months later the couple divorced. That wife had been sadly mistaken in the needs of her husband; he wanted more from his wife than booze and parties. Yet, to the outside world (and perhaps even to the wife) this marriage had seemed a complete success.

I recall a marriage that to those of us who knew the couple was almost perfect. The couple seemed tremendously happy. He shared gifts with his wife, he didn't criticize her in public, he seemed to understand her feminine peculiarities and moods and he would, by his actions, indicate to the neighbors that he loved his wife.

She was the perfect wife, one of the "old school." She pressed her husband's suits and shined his shoes so that in public he was neat and trim. She herself was personally attractive. She encouraged her husband to have male companionship even though she was left at home alone. She was an excellent cook; dinner was always ready when he returned home. She even went fishing with him though she had an aversion to worms and taking fish off hooks.

Suddenly, to the complete astonishment of all of us, that "perfect" marriage came to an end. The little town of fifteen hundred people, where everyone knew everyone else's business, was really shaken. Laura and Arthur separated. What had gone wrong? Family life, on the surface, was harmonious. Yet here was a marriage that went into a tailspin from which it never recovered. The couple eventually divorced.

We might indeed be surprised when a "good" marriage in our block or neighborhood or among our friends suddenly fails, yet we really should not be taken aback. Most people who are in the know on marriages, along with those who have made careful studies of the matter, will confirm that a so-called good marriage is more fragile than a bad one. That is because we make fantastic demands on our marriages. It is amazing how insidiously these unions are subjected to strain. Paradoxically, a good marriage has the possibility of failure because it is good.

TIMES HAVE CHANGED
It is hardly necessary to point out how marriages have been shot full of holes in these times. The institution itself is under microscopic scrutiny by psychiatrists, marriage counselors, and behavioral scientists.

In his best-selling book *Future Shock,* Alvin Toffler suggests that we shall see "serial marriages" in the near future. Under this concept, a young man or woman in love would have a trial marriage without children. Then if they decide to continue the union, they would have children together. If not, they would split up, marry others, and after a trial period have children with them. When the children of these marriages grew up, the couples might split it again and remarry for the childless years of their gathering old age.[1]

Benjamin Spock, the famed child specialist, doesn't feel this is such a bad idea. He believes that one of the more

---
[1] "Facing the Middle Age Crisis," *The National Observer* (Apr. 5, 1971), p. 12.

promising trends is that young people who are serious enough to marry are ready first to live together openly. This gives them, he says, an opportunity to find out whether they are really compatible and lessens the possibility that sexual attraction is the main thing drawing them together.

Now we might think that such changes in outlook would not affect those of us who are in middle age, but let's not kid ourselves. These concepts are throwing all kinds of doubts into existing marriages. We begin to wonder. Through the years we have thought of our particular marriage as deeply affectionate and full of meaning. We have looked forward to middle age and have realized that our marriage relationship was to become of greater importance to our emotional and mental well-being in the later years than when we were young and first married.

Then we read all about these new experiments in marriage, the new concepts, and we wonder. We wonder whether our marriage is really all that good or whether it has been dying right along and we didn't realize it. As a matter of fact, why would we want to read articles or books such as this one unless we had doubts or needed reassurance?

Times have changed the general concepts of marriage. For example, it is impossible for me to visualize the following hypothetical scene:

Frank: Let's sit down here and talk seriously about our marriage.
Julia: These have been the happiest years of our lives.
Frank: I think our marriage needs more action. It is not swinging enough!
Julia: Do you mean we should do more exciting things together—like taking long walks in the evening?
Frank: No. I mean in bed. We need more stimulation.

As I say, I simply cannot picture my father and mother sitting down to talk like this. Marriage to them was sacred; it was holy matrimony. It was more than just a civil or social arrangement. Being divinely bestowed, it was a union for life with permanence and exclusiveness. They never questioned it.

Today, with all of the so-called honesty we speak of in marriage, there is a good chance we can blow it completely apart. A man or woman today might think that honesty in marriage will improve it, but actually complete honesty might make it more difficult to endure. This is what prompted Jean Kerr to write to a wife who had been told by her husband that he had been cheating on her, "If he had the decency of a truck driver, he'd keep his lousy affair secret."

One psychiatrist squelches those who think that by middle age we have found love and that everything is beautiful. He says there is nothing beautiful about it; we are still looking for an ideal love. He tells us we are acting out fantasies and that all this joy in our marriage is hiding something dark and furtive in our relationship. Others say, "Take a good look at your marriage. If you have made a lousy life for yourself, make a change before you are too old to swing."

A couple was gloriously happy together until she went to a sensitivity group a friend recommended. There she met a number of men and women who indeed seemed contented. In due time she learned, through conversations with a married man she met there, that she really was not getting the fulfillment from her marriage that she had always thought she was getting. The idea was new to her, but the more she thought about it, the more she saw it could be true. She divorced her husband and married the friend of the encounter session. However, her newfound "happiness" that she so earnestly sought still eluded her. It is doubtful whether she ever will find it.

Richard Farson, a behavioral scientist, writes: "The values of the new consciousness emphasize honesty over loyalty or kindness. Honesty is rarely unadulterated, however, and all too often is used to alleviate guilt and transfer responsibility. It may help to remember that marriage, like any other important institution, needs some myth and mystique to keep it vital." [2]

OVERLY HIGH EXPECTATIONS

Dr. Spock has found that the older critics of marriage and the family seem to imply that they once had expected to have a glorious marriage bestowed on them as if it were a gift from God. Such was true in the cases of our mothers and fathers. But there is more to marriage than that. Dr. Spock says:

> Anyone who has a good marriage knows that he and his spouse had to work hard to make it good—and still have it. And work in this sense does not mean just toiling in the kitchen or office. It means to be sensitive to one's spouse, to listen, to try to understand his feelings, to wonder in a dispute whether he might be right and you might be wrong. It means generosity of spirit.[3]

In such a marriage there is a balance and a greater personal satisfaction in contributing rather than in receiving.

A similar view is expressed by Esther Oshiver Fisher, a counselor who holds a law degree and doctorate in education from Columbia University. She says that there is a "lack of commitment, an inability to take responsibility, to take on full partnership in many marriages."

One of the causes of marriage insecurity after the kids have left home is that we have not taken the time to see where our marriage has been going all along. We have been so busy with the kids, our jobs, and our personal

---

[2] Richard Farson, "Why Good Marriages Fail," *McCall's* (October 1971), p. 166. Used by permission.
[3] From "What Makes a Happy Family?" by Benjamin Spock, M.D., *Redbook*, November 1971, p. 68. Copyright © 1971 by The McCall Publishing Company. Used by permission.

affairs that we have failed to reassess our marriage. Unfortunately, we have been lulled into a kind of romanticism that comes from life around us; we have assumed that the "work" is no longer necessary.

All too often, television presents a highly romanticized view of family life, both in the daytime serial and in the evening family show. If these programs are taken merely for what they are—entertainment—little harm is done, but when they become models for real marriage, watch out. Let us consider, for example, a show which my family long enjoyed, *My Three Sons.* The TV family had problems, to be sure, but they seemed somewhat unreal. A pretty wife, a hard-working husband, and basically nice kids were portrayed. The wife always looked enticing whether in the bedroom or kitchen. While it is not good policy to go about with curlers in the hair, certainly there are times when wives are, and look, harried and untidy. Husbands definitely should be understanding and possess a sense of humor, but Fred MacMurray is unbelievable.

My children may visualize their future marriages as those depicted on the screen, while my wife and I originally conceived of our marriage as patterned after those of our parents. Changing times have altered our outlooks, it is true, but the fact is that marriage is for real and under the glamor and over-romanticizing remains the need for hard work.

WOMEN'S LIBERATION

Jessie Bernard, an authority on sex, marriage, and the family, has said:

> I believe too long women have allowed men exclusively to define sexuality, including female sexuality, to everyone's loss. Women are so accustomed to thinking about sex in male terms and from a male perspective and in terms of pleasing men that they have neglected to develop their own conception of themselves. I think we have all suffered from

this one-sided approach to sex and sexuality. . . . Now we learn that much of what we thought we knew is not correct. . . . I think it behooves women to correct the situation, to study themselves, to learn about themselves.[4]

In the November 1971 issue of *Holiday Inn* is an interesting quotation: "Most men believe a woman's place is in the home, and they expect to find her there immediately after she gets off work."[5] A man who seriously holds to this concept today may find his marriage in trouble.

Let us consider some extreme examples of "male chauvinism." When I was visiting in the Holy Land some years ago, I stopped at the tent of a Bedouin herdsman in the scrub area near the Dead Sea. I was invited into his tent to refresh myself. Stepping from the bright sunlight into the darkness, I almost stumbled over two large mounds of what appeared to be rags or clothing just inside the door. The host snapped his fingers. Tongue against teeth, he made two sharp hissing noises, then added some monosyllables of command. The mounds rose and scuttled out —they were his wife and his mother-in-law. They picked up two huge terracotta urns and set off into the scrub with the urns balanced on their heads. "They will bring fresh water," I was told. "The spring is only a mile away."

The women returned and my host poured water over my wrists and neck. "This will refresh you," he said as he kept pouring. I felt guilty as I thought about the distance the women had had to travel. He emptied one urn completely, and his wife began fixing coffee with the water in the other. Meanwhile the mother-in-law trudged off into the scrub to get another urn of water, a long mile away.

In the same country I saw a man riding his burro as his wife and goats trailed along behind. "Do you know why she is walking and he is riding?" asked my driver and

---

[4] Jessie Bernard, "Who/What Makes a Family Today?" *Lutheran Women* (November 1971), p. 6. Used by permission.
[5] *Holiday Inn* (November 1971), p. 40.

guide. I confessed ignorance on this point, and he said, "It's because that herdsman has only one burro."

While household responsibility in what we call the "modern world" is not this onerous, there is a striving on the part of both men and women to secure the acceptance of the proposition that women should have equal rights socially, politically, and economically. Men and women should have equal pay for equal work; equal opportunity in professions, commerce, and politics; equal rights in marriage and law. While social justice must become a reality for women, this does not mean that women are the same as men. There are emotional as well as the obvious physical differences.

Of late, women have become dissatisfied, and this is particularly evident after the kids have left home. A woman by this time may have worked at a full- or part-time job or have done volunteer service. Whether she has or not, she finds staying at home alone confining. She may go out into the world to find freedom from the stereotype of the "homebody." She may stay at home but chafe at the irritation of a seemingly "useless" day.

Richard Farson cannot explain why couples who fulfill their masculine and feminine roles get to a point where the marriage fails. Possibly it is because "they have come to see their marriage as symbolizing their slavery to these oppressive roles, or because their new understandings show their marriage to be so limiting that they can no longer live with the incongruity between what they have and what they feel they must have."[6]

CANDLELIGHT AND ROMANCE

One tendency of couples in middle age is to think too much about the past high points of their marriage as compared to the present. When they were young, the couple had resiliency and high hopes for the future. They had

---

[6] Farson, op. cit., p. 111.

time on their side. Courtship and the novelty of beginning a marriage cast a romantic aura about them. The coming of children might have been significant in the marriage relationship. Even the trials and tribulations, viewed from this later perspective, were fun to work out. Love conquered all.

By the time the empty-nest period has rolled around, the glamor of a marriage may have worn a trifle thin. We may feel time is no longer on our side, and physically we don't bounce back as quickly as we used to. There is a tendency to look back on the "good old days" and wonder where they have gone. But this kind of romanticizing won't do so far as the future is concerned. It is a new ball game and memories of romance and excitement in our youth can be detrimental for a middle-age marriage if we have not matured in our ideas.

THE VICE OF ADVICE

In an issue of a national magazine there was a letter to the "advisor." The writer, a woman, purports to be seeing a psychiatrist about some of her personal problems. She wrote that her counselor has suggested that he might better relate to her problems if he were to lie down on the couch next to her. Without going into further details, I would like to point out that unfortunately reading attention-getting material such as this can lead to confusion and give erroneous ideas. There is a great deal of such trash written. I have been in editorial work long enough to know that this type of letter is often staged—requested by the editor to fill up space or made up out of whole cloth for sensationalism. Unfortunately, publications with such material find their way into many homes. Not only do they give a misconception of what marriage and the ensuing problems are like but they can also breed uncertainty. We read of things we never would have thought of before.

Reading "advice" columns may be interesting and occasionally offers a thought or two worth considering. An over-active imagination and the desire of couples to have that "perfect" marriage of romantic dreams, however, may lead to a problem where none existed before or which might have been correctable through the use of common sense. Sometimes, as in the case of the advice columns, "a little knowledge can be a dangerous thing."

"KEEPING UP WITH THE JONESES"

Tom and Ruth have just stepped into the fifties. They are the parents of one son who recently completed college and lives in another state. They have always been close and get along well together. But lately there have been periods when Ruth, especially, has become depressed and unhappy. "I have the feeling that somehow I'm missing something . . . that my feet are caught in muck, and I just cannot move," she says.

Ruth looks around at her neighborhood, at the members of her club, at her associates at church and among her friends and she wonders, "Why are they all so happy and contented and I'm not?" She realizes she has much to be thankful for, but the feeling of discontent remains.

In conversation with one of the couples Tom and Ruth know, they are surprised to learn about all the fun things their friends have been doing. They listen attentively as Milt and Betty tell of their small cabin in the Catskills which they enjoy going to even during the cold winter weekends. There is a fireplace, and "we keep warm by sleeping in our clothes, getting some heat from the oven. It is so much fun to tramp in the snow, ski, and huddle up in that cabin" runs the enthusiastic account. Hearing this, Ruth wonders what other marriages are like. From conversation, she feels they must be filled with fun and excitement. In comparison, she and Tom seem to go along at a humdrum pace, concerned mainly with bills, the house, and an occasional "ordinary" vacation.

Ruth and Tom, and I suspect a good many others of us,

may not realize that there are façades, even unintentional ones, erected. For that matter, how does our own marriage appear to the world? We do not know, nor do we seek to know, what is actually going on. If we did, we would find that these other couples are concerned with the same or similar anxieties that we are. We might be surprised to learn that the contributing causes for strain on a fragile marriage—narcissism, hostility, willfulness—are present in other marriages too. Jealousy, the fear of losing one's mate to another, may be present.

In the book *Eleanor and Franklin* there is a provocative portion that deals with the affair between Franklin Roosevelt and his wife's onetime secretary, Lucy Mercer, later Lucy Mercer Rutherford. According to Joseph P. Lash, the author, Eleanor offered to divorce her husband because of his romance with Lucy. Mrs. Roosevelt had discovered the romance, according to the book, in 1918 after her then handsome, somewhat frivolous and flirtatious husband of thirteen years returned from Europe stricken with double pneumonia. It was during this period that Mrs. Roosevelt discovered Lucy's letters to Mr. Roosevelt.

Eleanor was prepared to give her husband his freedom, but he feared that his mother would cut him off from any inheritance and that his political career would be ended if there was a divorce. So for the remaining years, so far as the world was concerned, Eleanor and Franklin were a happily married couple who were able to overcome their problems. A façade had been erected.

We cannot assume that other marriages are better than our own. Other couples have the same trouble spots, periods when friction is likely to occur, and deep-rooted troubles on occasion. The façade is not important; the marriage itself is. In our concern that we have a "perfect" marriage, let's not sell ourselves short. Our concern is not the marriage of another couple and how we fall short of their "perfection," but rather what our own marriage is really like.

CROSSING THE FINISH LINE

Both my sons in high school and college have been involved in long-distance track events. As you can imagine, I have seen a good many meets and have watched the runners cross the finish line. Marriage in the middle years can be likened to a track meet. There is the warm-up period, the starting gun, the long run, and the finish line. By the time a couple reaches the middle years, they may find themselves regarding their marriage as having crossed the finish line. What remains seems anticlimactic.

Several generations ago, marriage was entered into for survival, security, and/or convenience. Today the situation has changed. We hear of couples who say they have entered into marriage for intellectual companionship. Others marry to be involved in warm intimate moments, shared values, and the experience of deep, romantic love.

On CBS there was a program that dealt with an American family that had every reason to be thankful except for one thing, which the program described as the "shudder of discontent." The husband had achieved success; he was a senior vice-president of a Detroit bank, his salary was more than adequate to meet his needs. Just ready to step into middle age, he was considered as having "arrived." He and his wife lived in a suburb where parents with similar goals as theirs had worked hard for their attractive homes, new cars, summer homes, good schools. The family had realized the fulfillment of their dreams, only to discover the inevitable flaws.

The husband commutes to the city where he now spends ten to twelve hours daily on his job. He feels his family does not understand the pressure of the grind, that they do not appreciate the sacrifice that has gone into achieving success. He is seldom at home. The wife likewise spends little time home. She attends sensitivity sessions and goes to her Junior League meetings. The household is efficiently run by hired personnel.

It is the wife who most obviously feels she has crossed

the "finish line." A long time ago she competed to get a good education, to get the right man, to obtain the best for her children. With the maturing of these children, she now has the feeling that there is nothing more to strive for. This feeling of her mission being accomplished is a source of discontent and dissatisfaction.

As Richard Farson says, "The trouble is that these higher order needs [companionship, intimate moments, shared values, deep romantic love, great sexual pleasure] are more complex and therefore less easy to satisfy on a continuing basis than are, say, financial needs. For this reason, they give rise to more frustrations and more discontent when they are not met." [7]

THE PROBLEMS OF SEX

The problem of sexual fulfillment, as is constantly proclaimed in books, in magazines, in newspapers, and on television, is a major source of discontent today among single, divorced, widowed, and married people.

Couples in the empty-nest period are not exceptions. We will deal in more detail with this aspect in a later chapter, but the point to be made here is that even in those marriages which up to now had seemed satisfactory, the partners learn that, contrary to the beliefs of earlier generations, sexual demands must be met even more completely and understandingly.

The amount of material on the subject of sex is overwhelming. A couple who innocently have been happy and contented through the years begins to wonder if they haven't been missing something. Persons who truly want to have a good marriage are especially vulnerable. No longer do they accept as a matter of course the vagaries, shortcomings, and frailties of their partners.

CONCLUSION

Oddly enough, the higher the ideal of marriage that is held up, the more subject that union is to the storms of

[7] Ibid.

everyday living and the changes of the times. With a firm foundation of understanding the stresses and with the application of common sense, the marriage endures.

Mentioned in this chapter have been the current outlook, expectations which are unattainable, the change in woman's place in society, an impractical romanticism, the dangers of shallow advice, a detrimental comparison of a couple's marriage with those of acquaintances, a feeling that goals have been reached and there is nothing worth working toward, and the strain of the current emphasis on sex. You can think of other insidious forces which assail the minds and lives of those who are serious in their search for a good marriage after the kids have left home.

2 THE GRASS LOOKS GREENER

In the eyes of those of us who knew him, Harry was a fine example of a family man. The only son of a couple who saw to it that he was raised "properly," Harry regularly was taken to church and church school as a youth. He was the pride of his father as he starred on the local high-school football team. Harry was offered numerous scholarships, but he chose a small Ohio college not far from home. There were many girls all too happy to be seen with the campus hero, but Harry chose Debbie, an attractive, vivacious girl. Following graduation, he and Debbie were married, and he went on to get a master's degree in education administration. He finally became the superintendent of schools in a large Ohio city. By the time Harry had reached middle age, his parents, Debbie, and their two teenage children had good cause to be proud of him.

Harry was a pillar at the United Presbyterian church. He was an able school administrator, welding the system into a well-organized unit.

One day, however, his mother tearfully brought me a letter she and her husband had received. Harry was in Las Vegas. He had ditched his job, his wife, and his two children (now in college) and had gone to Nevada with his administrative secretary, a woman fifteen years his junior. The revelation of the affair was a shock to everyone; no one had suspected a thing.

In later assessment of the weeks and months prior to Harry's "defection," changes in his personality were recalled. Apparently the press of duties involved longer and longer hours at work; his secretary stayed too. At school-board meetings his eyes would glaze with indifference where formerly he had been efficient and forceful. Sometimes he would get moody, then suddenly become ebullient. As an athlete he had passed up drinking and smoking, but now he fell back on both to steady his nerves and quiet his mind.

Harry really did not know what had gotten into him. Perhaps it was the introspection he found himself indulging in. On the surface, Debbie was still a great gal—good looking for a woman her age, intelligent, but a trifle dull at home. It was difficult to shake her loose from her usual routines and ideas. She did give in on the drinking question by taking a sip of sherry now and then, though she made it clear to everyone that she felt more comfortable with the effervescent bubbles of a soft drink.

Harry felt he cared for Debbie, but that knockout he worked with did something to his verve. At times Debbie let him falter sexually, but his secretary could send him up a wall as she sat near him with her dress, short enough to start with, creeping up. And that perfume—he would ask himself if now were not the time for him to escape the trap of his job and marriage and head west with Gloria. He wrestled with the problem of being a "dirty old man" or becoming "horny" on the occasional trips away from home.

Harry became a victim of the "middle-age crisis." Psychiatrists have only recently concerned themselves with "middle-age marriages." They have been so busy studying and writing books and articles about adolescence at one end of life and old age at the other that a vacuum has been created in between. One has only to glance through the "Dear Abby" columns to realize how many problems do occur in these "middle years." Prominent national leaders have made headlines when so-called "happy" marriages have gone awry. Psychiatrists and marriage counselors have discovered that the Harrys and Debbies are legion. Now, at last, we are beginning to realize that serious help is needed to save faltering marriages, or, even better, to prevent the marriages from faltering in the first place.

Bernice Neugarten, professor of human development at the University of Chicago, has been studying the problems of middle age. She says:

> Sure, who in the world hasn't been bored with one's mate at one time or another? But other things grow up in the course of time—call it sympathy, call it affection, call it old-fashioned love—and we're all wary of losing this. I don't think communal marriages and serial marriages are going to catch on. I don't think people are going to give up the need that we all have for the long term, intimate relationships. This is an enormous need, at all ages.[1]

Intimacy can be quickly attained, says Dr. Neugarten, but there is something to the idea of length. The truly liberated, educated man of middle age does not expect his mate to be the symbolic example of all virtues. "What I am saying, in a crude way, is that you can go to bed with someone but that somehow doesn't dismiss the need for a long-standing relationship."[2] Dr. Neugarten feels that it is good to go home to someone who has known you for twenty-five years. Probably there is no place like home—if there is sympathy and understanding there. That's what surprised the prodigal son—he expected a reprimand, but his father gave him a tender kiss.

THE SCOPE OF THE PROBLEM

Alvin Toffler, author of the best-seller *Future Shock,* has made some startling statements regarding the future of marriage and the family. His prognosis has caused us to sit up and take notice of what is going on in the home.[3]

Toffler says that the family is in for a severe upheaval for

---

[1] Quoted in Peter T. Chew, "Good Old Charlie and Faithful Jane," *The National Observer* (Apr. 5, 1971), p. 12. Used by permission.
[2] Ibid.
[3] "The American Family," *Look* (Jan. 26, 1971), p. 35.

27

at least two reasons: scientific developments and social mobility. Discoveries leading to a biological breakthrough are liable to have a shattering effect on marriage and the family. The wide use of the "pill" and the continual improvements in its use will result in all kinds of changes in the style of living between both married and unmarried couples. But the first impact of the "pill," says Toffler, will be like a popgun compared to the howitzers and the nuclear weaponry that lie ahead in the field of biology. For years now we have been reading about Italian and Russian scientists, as well as those in the United States, who are able to develop babies in test tubes. Artificial insemination not only is a reality among cows but also has become a method for securing children in otherwise childless families. The church and society have already been wrestling with the multitude of problems raised by such methods of conception.

The possibility of programing children so that their characteristics may be determined before birth is not so far away. Studies have been made to determine if parents might choose the sex of their child before it is born.

In addition to biological changes, the economic and social structure of the family has altered as well. Consider the matter of mobility. On the street where I have lived for eight years, there are only three families who have been there as long as we. The others have moved to such far-away places as Europe or to various sections of the country. When I have talked to the real estate dealers, they have surprised me with the report that our community—considered fairly stable—is constantly in a state of flux.

The mass exodus from rural to metropolitan areas, the frequent transfer of personnel by corporations, the convenience of the automobile and the highways have contributed to the character of family life. When I was a kid, about all we could afford to do so far as mobility was concerned was walk to the local ball park to watch the Sunday afternoon baseball games and then get together with friends and relatives who lived nearby. For a treat, the family might travel by car twenty or thirty miles to some point of interest. Today my family is scattered all over the world. My sister lives in Japan with her family, my married son is in North Carolina, and various aunts, uncles, and cousins live in Oregon, Texas, Arizona, Indiana, and Ohio.

John Platt, associate director of the University of Michigan's Mental Health Research Institute, says, "All sorts of roles now have to be played by the husband and wife, whereas in the older, extended family they had all sorts of help—psychological support, financial support and so on. The pressures of these multiple roles are partially responsible for the high rates of divorce, alcoholism, tranquilizers and so on."[4]

In the past, an outcome of marriage was the bearing of children. Today there are those who predict that there may be a great deal of childlessness in various segments of society.

Less than a hundred years ago when the preacher, together with the bride and groom, intoned "until death do us part," that meant, barring unforeseen illness or accident, about thirty years, with an occasional golden wedding anniversary. Today the fifty-year celebration is more frequently celebrated, as can be seen in newspapers. Longevity has increased and so far as their life spans are concerned, a couple can make their marriage a binding covenant for at least two generations.

So we have mass mobility and changes in neighborhoods, sex patterns, and leisure time. As Toffler points out, "all of these feed into society and make it more difficult for two people in love to grow together. Each of them is exposed to more and more experiences that are different from the other's, with the consequence that the ideal of a

---

[4] "The American Family: Future Uncertain," *Time* (Dec. 28, 1970), p. 35. Used by permission of Dr. Platt.

couple's growing together through the years becomes increasingly remote."[5]

He feels that there will be a shift to more temporary marital arrangements, an intensification of the present patterns of divorce and remarriage, and divorce and remarriage to the point where we accept the idea that marriages are not for life. "I'm not endorsing it," says Toffler, "but I think it is likely to be the case."

NEW CONCEPTS BUT STILL THE TRADITION

With prominent Americans such as Alvin Toffler making not too incomprehensible predictions, we can visualize what we are in for so far as marriage and the family are concerned. Marriages taking place today are in for some changes, to say the least.

Some of these marriages are already unusual. In La Jolla, California, Michael, an oceanographer, and his artist wife Karen, both twenty-seven, had been married for four years when Michael met Janis, who was studying at the Scripps Institute of Oceanography. Janis often came to study at Michael and Karen's apartment so that a strong attachment developed. When Michael took off for Antarctica, the two women developed a close friendship and both decided they loved Michael. They thought all three should be able to live amicably together. Last year the trio formalized it all with an improvised wedding ceremony.

They were all delighted to learn that Karen was pregnant. "We'll all take turns caring for the baby," says Janis, "just as we all share the household chores. That way each of us has time for the things we like to do the best."[6]

This is an extreme or way-out experiment in marriage, yet consider the way communes are springing up all over America. A few years ago we might have heard of groups

---

[5] Alvin Toffler, *Future Shock* (New York: Random House, 1971), ch. 11. Copyright © 1970 by Alvin Toffler. Used by permission.
[6] *Time*, loc. cit., p. 38.

of long-haired persons living together, but now organization has crept in. In Warwick, Massachusetts, "The Brotherhood of the Spirit" was recently organized. It has drawn 160 seekers of peace, regeneration, and understanding. There is "no booze, no drugs, no promiscuity, lots of soap and water, kindness, trust, and sharing of labor" in this commune. In addition, we hear of "swinger" parties in various cities and wife-swapping in some neighborhoods.

It is obvious that all kinds of changes in families and marriages are taking place in our society. To speak of these changes in a book such as this seems futile. How can one spark a marriage in a society that is undergoing such revolutions in the concepts of marriage and family? There is an answer. While certain unusual occurrences taking place now become more frequent—and no doubt will continue to do so in the coming years—there are millions of marriages, traditional in most senses of the word, that need to be dealt with now. These are the marriages that took place in the 1940's and early 1950's where the couples now are confused and unhappy over changes they see taking place in their own marriages. They do not crave communal living or even wife-swapping, but they do not understand what is happening to what they thought was a good partnership.

According to national statistics, the period twenty-five to twenty-nine years after the wedding is one of the times that the traditional marriage is most threatened. Then the rate of divorce registers as high as 36 percent.[7] The family cycle period most affected by this situation is when the adolescents run away from home (a half million do this every year), when they leave for college or employment, or when they marry.

However necessary or common these events may be, they can be traumatic, and not only to the young people. I

---

[7] Betty Rollin, "The American Way of Marriage: Remarriage," *Look* (Sept. 21, 1971), p. 62.

recall the time nearly thirty-five years ago when I left for college. My parents waved good-by as they stood on the front steps, tears streaming down their faces. Today our emotions might not be so obvious, the family unit may not be so tightly knit, and modern means of travel have shortened distances, but the emotional wrench is still there. As I see my own children marry or leave for college, I realize that our home life will never be quite the same. The kids do come home on vacations and we can visit them in their new abodes, but they will more than likely never stay at home again.

This period of living together as man and wife may become more difficult than the earlier years. When the children were young and growing up there were the trials and excitement of rearing the family, a preoccupation with music lessons, ball games, school events, church programs. Though we possibly viewed ourselves at times as slaves with little time for ourselves or we may have looked forward to the time when the seemingly endless demands would cease, we were appalled when it actually arrived. As the family leaves home, middle age may be a continuation of the great days of earlier years, a fulfillment and joy in each other's companionship, or a period of passive mediocrity and dissatisfaction, even if there is no divorce or separation.

PHYSICAL CHARACTERISTICS OF MIDDLE AGE
Creeping upon us are physical changes so gradual we are almost unaware of them. An ad published by the President's Council of Physical Fitness and Sports says, "There is no such thing as stylishly stout." The battle of the pot—and I don't mean drugs—all too often hits men at middle age. The belly expands further and further over the belt. We try diets and knock off a few pounds only to fall back into our old eating habits and discover that our excess poundage is once again with us. The realization that we can no longer wear the up-to-date styles comes as a blow.

How do flare pants look with a forty-six plus flare at the top? How about trying to get that tapered shirt past the "hump" line? There are other signs. The golfer realizes that at the fifteenth hole, if not sooner, he has run out of steam. The weekend tennis enthusiast can no longer play as many sets as he once did. The football player discovers that it is easier to watch the game on television than to participate in a pick-up game of touch football. Suddenly one realizes he has a mouthful of cavities filled with silver, or gold if he can afford it. Possibly there are dentures. Bifocals are a part of vision now, and a hearing aid may be concealed in one's glasses. All of this is a matter for humor, until one realizes it applies to him.

What about the embarrassing experiences which arise from being unable to recall names? A momentary lapse of memory reminds one that later may come such disquieting episodes as a fluttering heart or moments of sexual impotency.

For the man, these represent the disappearance of youth and with it the degree of physical buoyancy he once enjoyed. His greatest sexual pleasure is gotten from looking at a copy of *Playboy*. The changes, or rather the realization of these changes, put a burden on marriage and the mate whether we like it or not. The husband may become like Harry, infatuated with younger women, some no older than his own daughter. Now is the time for the man to reassess his capabilities or realign his habits or trends of thought.

The woman does not escape the changes either, though she may be more clever in concealing them. When Marjorie, my wife, first noticed those gray hairs, she carefully plucked them out. But with the appearance of more and more, she has finally done what millions of other American women are doing—she headed to "Joseph's" for a return to her "natural" color. Nevertheless, she knows the gray is still there. Calorie charts appear in the kitchen and scales are conspicuous in the bathroom.

33

From forty to the middle fifties women go through the menopause period when certain psychological factors need sympathetic understanding. The ovaries atrophy and consequently the monthly cycle of menstruation ends, and with it ovulation. This period of transition may be accompanied by depression and even a feeling of despair and uselessness on the part of the woman when she loses her reproductive capacity. A similar feeling is involved when a woman undergoes a complete hysterectomy. Some married women become so up-tight as a result of these factors that they find it impossible to respond adequately to sexual acts. Women who have never received much satisfaction from their sexual relations with their mates may use this period to dispense with it altogether.

In middle age a woman may find herself with time on her hands. The children are away from home, errands are fewer, and there is less manual work to do at home. Modern appliances have lessened the working hours. With too much time, a woman may become bored and actual physical problems may result. Some choose this time to develop a mania for shopping which seems to fulfill an unsatisfied need to keep busy. Food, trinkets, and clothes are substituted for love. The worst thing that a woman in such a state can acquire is several charge accounts. Before anyone realizes it, financial problems can develop, putting still more of a strain on the marriage. With Dagwood and Blondie it is a joke, but the situation is not so funny to the man trying to meet those monthly bills. Of course, in such a case one might do as my friend John advised. He cajoled his wife into going to work. "This way," he confided, "I know she isn't out in some department store shopping for the bargains we don't need." However, even the working wife is not entirely immune from boredom or compulsive "bargain shopping."

A woman who does not succumb to the wiles of advertising may turn to verbally assaulting her husband. She is vaguely dissatisfied and, though she actually may have no such intentions, finds herself taking it out on her mate. The image of decorum to her friends and society as a whole, she becomes a veritable virago at home.

A conversation I overheard in the subway recently illustrates the point. One man asked, "How was your weekend?"

The other unburdened himself. "It's my wife. Friday night she started nagging me. Saturday she nagged all day. Sunday started the same. Finally I let her have it on Sunday night. What a bastard she is to live with!"

ADJUSTING TO THE PROBLEM

Middle-age couples who truly desire to keep their union alive and interesting sometimes find themselves at a loss as to how to proceed. Marriages being made up of individuals who vary in many ways, the solutions to problems are certainly not stereotyped or even easy to find. Marriage is a personal thing, and personalities must be considered. However, there are a few generalized and advance adjustments that can be made.

1. Avoid shriveling up in past memories or "the good old days." Time moves ahead. If you *must* talk about your World War II experiences, find an old army buddy. Unfortunately, there won't be too many others interested.

2. Add new satisfactions and challenges to your life. Expand your interests. Be optimistic. Do creative things. You will only find yourself deeper in the morass and a blue funk if you wake up every morning believing the world is in bad shape.

3. Sleep in the same bed or at least the same room as your spouse. So one of you snores? Get earplugs. A little space between a man and wife is not so bad, but a whole wall? Watch out! It's hard to make up when you are rooms apart.

4. Avoid running to the kids, whether married or single, with your problems. They have plenty of their own. Furthermore, they are likely to think less of you for your ina-

bility to be mature enough to cope with your own lives. It is quite likely that the generation to which your children belong will be a stranger to yours. Maintain a positive relationship with your children.

5. Keep loose and flexible. This will help you avoid a great deal of bickering. Be prepared to change your spending, working, and vacationing habits.

3 KEEP THE LINES OPEN

Most New Yorkers did not notice it, but one alert reporter was observant. During a wildcat strike that tied up the subways just at rush hour, the hurried, harried thousands pushed down the long stairs to the silent underground stations, were turned back at the toll gates, and then pressed back upstairs to seek some surface transportation. No one in the ascending stream told anyone in the descending stream on the same staircase that it was pointless to go all the way down. And none of those going down asked anyone going up why they were so suddenly turned around. To have communicated so, commented the reporter, would have violated New York's unwritten law that no one speaks to anyone else lest he be considered some sort of a freak or masher. So the morose masses slogged through the same mistake, hundreds by hundreds.

This lack of simple communication is so often the basis of many of our problems. The act of "making known" or "being connected," communication, is a necessity in many areas of life and especially in marriage if the marriage is to have meaning and to bring satisfaction to its partners. Communication may be verbal or emotional, but the important thing is that the lines of understanding be kept open. Some fortunate marriages have no problems in this regard. Man and wife have kept the channels open and when difficulties arise can solve them easily by talking with each other. Other marriages show little or no communication and an "I-you" relationship develops instead of a "we-our" partnership. The result is not necessarily divorce or separation, but it certainly does follow that the couple is in for numerous acts of unresponsiveness, misunderstandings, and disagreements, some of them fatal to the marriage bond.

Various causes can lead to a breakdown in communication—sometimes a combination of causes—but if the couple is serious about reestablishing a close relationship and is willing to go beyond mere wishful thinking, they can do so. All too often the problem of understanding each other surfaces after the children have left home and the husband and wife are thrown upon their own resources whereas before their family had provided a type of "buffer zone" and the differences were not so noticeable.

One cause of blocked communication is personality differences. For example, one partner may be talkative and outgoing while the other is laconic and withdrawn. It is possible that this very difference is what drew them together in the first place, but without understanding between the two, problems can arise in later years.

> When John Lardner's father [Ring Lardner, the famed short-story writer] wrote about married people, they were usually the kind who lived quarrelsomely ever after, and so he gave his stories ironic names like "The Love Nest." John Lardner's marriage was from those pages. But he and his wife, Hazel Belle Jean Cameron Lardner, a former secretary to the editor of the New York *Herald Tribune,* had an arrangement worked out whereby as Kahn [Roger Kahn, who was sports editor of *Newsweek*] puts it, "They didn't trespass on each other's territory." That meant that he didn't go to her bar and she didn't go to his. . . .
>
> John and Hazel's daughter, Susan, says of her mother's and father's marriage, "There was certainly a lot of tension. The responsibility for the difficulties was about evenly divided." Susan remembers her mother as "very outgoing, sociable, gregarious and lively." She remembers her father as just the opposite. John Lardner was so private that she never remembers his mentioning his own father. "We never initiated a

conversation with him," the daughter says. "We were conditioned not to ask questions."

Susan remembers sitting one night with her father, mother, brother, and sister. Her mother kept attempting the impossible: to make John Lardner talk. With each rebuffed effort she became more furious. Her temper came to a lively boil near the end of the meal. Susan says, "She threw a lamb chop bone at my father and grazed his forehead." Even then John Lardner said nothing.[1]

Still another situation affecting communication is the difference in occupations, a condition obviously present in many cases. A young married couple whom I visited were discussing family backgrounds. The wife said, "My father was terribly uncommunicative. He was so wrapped up in his job that he would leave for his office early in the morning, come home for lunch and barely say a word, leave again and arrive home in time for supper. Then he read the paper or a book and went to bed. Sometimes in all of this routine we would be lucky to get a grunt or two from him. Many of our meals were eaten in complete silence. I usually saw him give a perfunctory kiss to my mother three times a day—when he left in the morning, when he came home at night, and when he went to bed." In the father's job, it was revealed, he had to talk to people all day long. The mother, on the other hand, had been at home most of the day. The mother and father had remained together, but was there communication?

Astronaut Michael Collins, speaking at a banquet, stated that the average man speaks 25,000 words a day and the average woman, 30,000. Then he added, "Unfortunately, when I come home each day I've spoken my 25,000—and my wife hasn't started her 30,000."[2]

---

[1] Aaron Latham, "The Lardners: A Writing Dynasty," *The New York Times Magazine* (Aug. 22, 1971), pp. 10f. © 1971 by The New York Times Company. Reprinted by permission.
[2] *Reader's Digest* (June 1971), p. 118.

While the astronaut was jesting, it is a fact that there is an element of truth in what he said. Husbands and wives can be absolutely great in communicating at their places of business yet when they get home the conversation for the evening adds up to only a few hundred words.

Perhaps the middle-age couple does speak to each other frequently, carrying on perfunctory conversations. But is this necessarily communication? Hearing and listening are two entirely different things. We *hear* the street noises, the noises of factories, automobiles, the conversations of strangers or even of our own families, and yet we do not listen. It is as if we turn off a mental hearing aid. The illustration is given of a mother who lived in an apartment on a busy street corner. At night the sound of traffic never bothered her, and she slept soundly. But when her child in the next room cried softly in his sleep, she was at his side in an instant. We need to set our minds to listening, not merely hearing what our spouse is saying. The habit of non-listening can begin after the marriage and continue to the end of it. By the time the couple reaches middle age this habit may have developed greatly. A cartoon shows a wife and husband at the breakfast table, his head buried in his newspaper. She, with a look of exasperation, says, "John, I think I'll go to the grocery and to the library and then commit suicide." He replies without looking up, "Yes, dear, that would be nice. Have a good time." We smile, yet how much do *we* really *listen* to what is being said?

In the lyrics of the song by Simon and Garfunkel, "The Dangling Conversation," we find expressed an idea that could be applied to couples who no longer have open communication lines and are wistfully aware of their lack.

> It's a still-life water color of a now late afternoon
> As the sun shines through the curtain lace and shadows wash the room;
> And we sit and drink our coffee, couched in our indifference

Like shells upon the shore; you can hear the ocean roar
In the dangling conversation and superficial smiles,
The borders of our lives.

And you read your Emily Dickinson and I my Robert Frost
And we note our place with bookmarkers that measure what we've lost;
Like a poem poorly written, we are verses out of rhythm,
Couplets out of rhyme in syncopated time,
And the dangling conversation and the superficial smiles
Are the borders of our lives.

Yes, we speak of things that matter with words that must be said.
Can analysis be worthwhile? Is the theater really dead?
And how the room is softly faded and I only kiss your shadow,
I cannot feel your hand; you're a stranger now unto me
Lost in the dangling conversation and superficial smiles
In the borders of our lives.[3]

There is another type of major breakdown in communication which occurs when the message sent is not the message received.

A wife greets her husband with the words, "It's about time you got home." The husband, possibly tired from a hard day's work, hears the words but may get several messages. He might think she has all sorts of stored up "bad news" to impart and in his already weary condition feels he cannot endure any such recital. He is defensive, wanting *her* to deal with the problems and not bother him. Happily, he might interpret her words as showing her eagerness to see him again because she has missed him during the day and longs for his companionship. In this case he may respond with a caress or an embrace. If he has heard the same words for many years, he possibly may

[3] Simon and Garfunkel, "The Dangling Conversation," Columbia Records. © 1966 Paul Simon. Used with permission of Charing Cross Music, Inc.

shrug them off and say nothing. What makes a difference in the way the words are received? The tone of the voice, the facial expression, the position of the body, and the mood of the listener all enter into the interpretation.

On the other side of the coin, the wife may have had a particularly rough day when nothing seemed to go right or when problems have piled up on her. If her husband enters and at once says, "Is dinner ready yet?" she too may defensively feel that he is criticizing her for not attending to her wifely duties. Of course, there is always the possibility that he will use the opportunity to suggest going out to eat since dinner is not ready, but this, we admit, is not likely. She might also interpret his remark as inquiring whether or not he will have time to relax a while before dinner. Again, many elements affect the message received.

The story has gone the rounds about a housewife whose husband came home from work and always asked, "What's new?" To give him an answer that was unusual and different, she went out and bought a horse and put it in the bathtub. When he came home that night she received the surprise of her life. He said, "Would you like to go out to dinner and the theater tonight?" She had been reading him all wrong!

Communication is a two-way affair. When a husband steps in the door, he should be alert for both verbal and non-verbal messages, and the wife, likewise, should endeavor to catch his communication. "The ability to communicate in mutually affirming ways is the fundamental skill which is essential to the growth of marital intimacy. Marriage provides an opportunity for multilevel exchanges of meaning. It provides the opportunity for communicating at increasingly deep levels about the things that matter most to husband and wife." [4]

---

[4] Howard J. and Charlotte H. Clinebell, *The Intimate Marriage* (New York: Harper & Row, 1970), p. 89.

TRANSMISSION LINES

As mentioned earlier, it is well to remember that messages between a married couple can be sent in a variety of ways. By the time the middle years roll around there are ample opportunities to practice once again the old technique of saying, "No matter what happens, I love you and care for you." Both husband and wife can do some thoughtful things to express this mood—sharing a fond glance, listening with interest and without interruption to one's mate, bringing home an unexpected gift (please, not a new fishing reel when she has expressed no interest in catching, fixing, or eating fish), playfully pinching or touching a sensitive spot, nibbling the ear lobes, kissing the back of the neck, wearing a new perfume, placing a bowl of flowers on the table, eating in the dining room instead of the kitchen, building a fire in the fireplace on a cold evening, using a double bed instead of twin beds, calling in the middle of the day, eating dinner in a restaurant that has romantic atmosphere, or leaving the lights on instead of off in the bedroom when making love. Volunteering (not waiting to be asked) to do some little job one knows his spouse dislikes (i.e., taking out the trash, feeding the dog, cleaning shoes, washing dishes, returning a defective purchase to a store) touches a responsive chord without much being said verbally. Any of these gestures can heighten communication and invigorate a marriage. Few husbands or wives outgrow a weakness for such allures.

While we are discussing various ways of communication, we also must recognize that there are times when a person would like to be uncommunicative for a while, some individuals more than others. This is a natural feeling if the silence does not last for a long period of time or is not used as a punitive weapon. If someone is unusually tired, depressed, or momentarily irritated by something, silence may result. Exercise patience in such times and wait for the silence to pass.

William Lederer and Don Jackson feel that communications which have broken down physically can indeed be repaired. If both spouses agree to improve their communication, there is a small, seemingly elementary exercise which may help.

Mr. Lederer and Dr. Jackson suggest that the listener acknowledge the message of the speaker, then the speaker acknowledge the message of the listener. For example:

Mary: How blue the sky is today. (The original statement)

John: Yes, it certainly is a beautiful blue. (Acknowledgment that he has heard)

Mary: I'm glad you like it too. (Acknowledgment of John's statement)

Normally, such statements as Mary's invite a barely audible grunt or a shrug of the shoulders if there is any acknowledgment at all. Even worse might be the comment: "You idiot! Any fool can see the sky's blue today."

Implicit in this exercise is the attempt of each partner to let the other know he has been heard. Not only does the reticent one need to vocalize, but the loquacious one also curtails his verbosity and listens. Patience is the keyword!

LISTEN

On a Tuesday night television program, *Cimarron Strip,* the hero of the story, Scotty MacGregor, and Sarah Lou Burke are shackled together as they escape the verdict of the kangaroo court. He tells her, "The first thing a lady must learn to do is to listen to a gentleman." This is true so far as it goes, but the gentleman must also listen to the lady.

The fine art of listening needs cultivating. Test yourself by recalling the last time you went to a lecture or heard a sermon in church. Did you understand the beginning? Were you alert at the end? Were you mentally noting the main points? You would not be unusual if your mind wandered at intervals as you made an outward attempt to listen. You might have thought about the kids away at college or your visit to the married son or daughter. You might have been wondering about dinner, whether or not you remembered to turn on the oven for the roast, whom you should invite to the party next week, or what tomorrow at work would bring.

When I was in the pastorate, I had a veterinarian in one of my congregations who would quite often have to make a "house call" at an early hour on cold Sunday mornings. Shortly after he settled down in the pew for the church service he was dozing. The warm church and soft music helped him relax. So I am sure he heard very little of my sermon, even though his wife occasionally elbowed him sharply. But what was so unusual was that as we shook hands at the door following the service, he would always say, "I really enjoyed your sermon this morning." This is probably quite true. He did enjoy that opportunity to close his weary eyes, though he heard little or nothing of what I said.

Sometimes marriage is like that. Physically we are present, but we do not hear the words. A marriage becomes shaky when neither man nor wife really knows what the other has said. "Communication is the core of any successful marriage. When a couple loses the ability to reach each other with words and to really listen to each other, they are in deep trouble."[5]

Let's go a step farther on this matter of listening. We are not talking now about surface listening but rather about hearing the deeper meanings. Such listening is understanding what another person is trying to tell us even when he does not fully understand it himself. This attitude of feeling is called empathy, "the walking a while in the other man's moccasins." The word itself comes from

---

[5] Rebecca Liswood, *First Aid for the Happy Marriage* (New York: Trident Press, 1965), p. 161.

the Greek meaning "in suffering." One projects his own consciousness into another person's.

Empathy is an expression of the ability of married partners to feel the needs and problems of each other so that difficulties assume a new dimension. Listening in depth is not an easy thing. Each human has his or her share of emotions, prejudices, needs, and habitual attitudes. He is a person, not a stereotype. It is easy enough to moralize, advise, criticize, or utter words betraying indifference or hostility. In giving oneself to another person, however, one can uncover a whole new feeling that comes with the depth that should be a part of marriage. "It has been fully confirmed that when people have been able to unburden themselves of their intense and conflicting feelings then, and only then, do they become able to 'see' and to respond to 'sweet reason.' "[6]

TELL IT LIKE IT IS

A step toward good communication is to tell it like it is. After you wave goodbye to "little Bobby," who happens to be six feet tall by now and a real ox, the last of the children, you feel a twinge of emotion. Mama and Papa might be crying or sighing with relief, depending on the situation. The next morning they are squirting grapefruit in each other's eyes, alone for the first time since their oldest child made his first appearance. The buffers—the children—are gone.

Several days after Bobby has gone off to seek his fortune out in the cold, cruel world, Mama and Papa start getting frank with each other. The wife says, "You know, Hank, I've put up with it all these years, but that cross-stitch sampler your grandmother gave us, the one that says 'Bless, O Lord, This Happy Home' which you hung in

---

[6] William L. Carrington, *The Healing of Marriage* (Great Neck, N.Y.: Channel Press, 1961), p. 40.

the vestibule is positively an abomination to me! It looks dreadful. I want you to take it down."

Hank gets the message. He turns livid and is temporarily speechless. He always thought she regarded the sampler as highly as he did. He says bitterly, "Well, while we are having home truths around here, let me tell you a thing or two. I resent your handling our finances for the past twenty-five years. I've never even seen my pay checks. Furthermore, the sampler would look a lot better if the rest of the house were clean."

This touches a sore spot. "So you think so. Well, I'm sick of doing all the thinking and planning around here. Do you think it's fun making out our income tax and paying those bills you run up because you see a 'bargain'? How many bars of soap and jars of coffee do we have in the pantry, all bargains? We have enough toothpaste to brush the teeth of a herd of rhinoceros for a year. Furthermore, who has had to cope with the children all these years? Who played taxi for them and saw to it that they were properly dressed?"

And so it goes, on and on, with recriminations moving further and further from the point. All these years of harbored resentment have caused the explosion. Why had they not told each other of their real feelings about certain things before this?

When we tell it straight and do not harbor such resentments, it will be better for us in the long run. It is difficult to have communication when the people involved do not want to be seen as they really are or do not want to express their innermost thoughts and feelings. They resort to euphemisms.

James Farmer tells the story about a woman who had come into a great amount of wealth and wanted to record her family history. She engaged a writer for this very purpose. On checking out the family tree, the writer discovered that one of the woman's grandfathers had been electrocuted in Sing Sing's famous chair. The author said he had to be true to his integrity and include the fact in the genealogical record. The wealthy woman pleaded that he somehow take the sting out of this blot on her family history. When the record finally appeared, it stated, "One of her grandfathers occupied the chair of applied electricity in one of America's best known institutions. He was very much attached to his position and literally died in the harness." [7]

Marriage communication can be just as ambiguous. We try to hide reality and make things appear different from what they are. Candor and frankness are preferred unless an issue becomes so complicated that outside counsel is needed.

ACCESSIBILITY

It is all very well to talk of communication, but what happens when one or both partners in a marriage are inaccessible to each other from choice, whether consciously or subconsciously? A middle-age couple whose youngest daughter had recently married planned to take a vacation together in New England. The wife had greatly anticipated this week when she felt she and her husband would become closer together. But what happened when they arrived at their rented cabin? Did they take walks in the woods? Did they take advantage of a nearby lake by going boating and swimming together? Were there plans made to enjoy each other's companionship to the fullest? The wife commented to a friend after they returned home that her husband, though he was on vacation, would get up at 5 A.M. and sit in the car, dictating business letters all morning. In the afternoon he read or wrote reports. This continued all week. She was miserable, and I'm not sure it was a rewarding vacation for him. He wound up in the hospital with an ulcer, and she felt the week had been wasted.

[7] Ralph McGill, *Atlanta Constitution* (Apr. 24, 1968), p. 1.

Husbands and wives can make themselves inaccessible by created "busyness." A friend of mine, a professor at New York University, had a hard and fast rule in his home. "I don't want to be interrupted when the door to my study is closed," he announced firmly. He usually retired to the study at 8 A.M. and remained there until noon. The time in the afternoons and evenings when he was not teaching he made accessible to his wife. One day she had a desperate emergency that could not wait until noon. She felt she must violate the "closed door" policy. Hesitating, she opened the door and walked into the sanctum sanctorum only to find her husband practicing with his yo-yo!

Some of our "busyness" is about as foolish. We could make ourselves more accessible if we really wanted to. The "conscientious" husband or wife brings home a briefcase full of papers, hides in the study or bedroom, and continues his work. Others, not so conscientious and feeling a need for relaxation, head for the golf course, tennis court, or bowling alley. There is nothing wrong with an occasional night out, but when every night and even weekends are so occupied, something is wrong.

In contemporary American life the "boob tube" makes for inaccessibility. Brains are hypnotized and fantasy lives substituted for reality. Conversation is practically nil. Such living is a drug, as habit forming and enervating as any weed, mushroom, or poppy. The values promoted are those of self-indulgence and status, not of accomplishment and the satisfaction of first-hand experience. Communication is stifled.

Let us suppose that a middle-age couple does find a program they both enjoy. They sit together, holding hands or nibbling a snack in the evening as they watch it. But what kind of togetherness is it when commercials constantly interrupt? They are reminded graphically of bad breath, foul waves emanating from the armpits, teeth that must be soaked in a blue wash overnight, and the need for a sixty-second workout on a scalp that long ago saw the hair disappear down the drain.

Be accessible for communication. Both husbands and wives need to learn how important this is. If you are separated all day, how about a cup of coffee, tea, fruit punch, or other libation together when you return home? Why not take a break during the evening, with no television, papers, or magazines to interfere, to talk about the day's events. Each family has some tough decisions to make and problems to face so the husband and wife must set aside time to be together.

Some say structured plans to communicate are too mechanical to be effective. But once the techniques are learned, the reaction can be spontaneous. My sons had a hard time learning the fundamentals of golf; their balls would go all over the course, usually landing in the water hazards. But as they continued to play, the various rules of the game became natural, and now the "old man" has trouble keeping up with them. Practice will make for a better utilization of the moments of accessibility in the same way. A word of caution is necessary. Each conversation need not be a time of soul-searching or a no-holds-barred verbal slugfest. You are not in a confessional booth; you are not playing psychoanalyst. Rather, keep the conversations warm, friendly, and straightforward. Keep loose. In a cartoon of a man and wife marooned on a desert island, he is saying, "Our marriage counselor will be pleased. We're on a continuing dialog!" Such a predicament is not wished on anyone; communication can become a reality under far less drastic circumstances.

If something troublesome does emerge from these times of conversation which cannot be handled by the couple, they should meet with a qualified clergyman or marriage counselor who, in turn, may suggest further sources of help.

SOMETHING TO STEER BY

Everyone has suggestions for the improvement of listening between husband and wife. If you wish to follow some new forms and exercises for communication, here are a few suggested by marriage counselors and leaders of encounter groups:

1. *Listen carefully to the words of "The Dangling Conversation" by Simon and Garfunkel.* Discuss them. What positive action can they lead to?

2. *Have an "alone time."* Look into each other's eyes for a full minute. Repeat the name of your spouse several times as you look at each other, flexing your voice. Convey a message of love.

3. *Learn to listen with the "inner ear."* Search for meanings which might not be verbalized. By adding what we do not hear to what we do hear, we become much more sensitive in our communication.

4. *Listen without interrupting.* Interruptions cut off what the individual is trying to say and his meaning becomes unclear. We say, "I'm not interested in what you are saying" when we do not allow him to complete what he has to say.

5. *Keep your cool when you listen.* Our anger, self-interest, or excitement may keep us from tuning in to the other person. (See the chapter, "Let's Quarrel Constructively.") It might be a good idea to settle down, arrange for privacy, or concentrate on hearing the opposite viewpoint. Calmness is especially desirable if your wife comes in to tell you she has put the first dent in your new $3,000 automobile.

6. *Do not fake listening.* Such insincerity is soon found out.

7. *Try the touch method.* Spontaneous physical contact can help to get a message through. Young people are freer in this respect, but why do we middle-age couples have to give them a priority on this kind of communication?

8. *Hold hands as you face each other.* Use the eye contact and repeat each other's name. Now stop holding hands and use some other way to communicate.

9. *Use a trust exercise such as blindfolding your mate and leading him or her around.* Do not consider this a party game but rather a time to explore feelings.

10. *Lie on your stomach and let your mate give you a body massage.* It's a good moment to relax and talk.

11. *Embrace.* There is nothing so beautiful and beautifully human as to be held, hugged, loved, to feel the warmth and sincerity of another person. Remember how you did it during courtship and soon after marriage? Words can deceive, but an embrace conveys a truth in which sound becomes secondary.

4 KEEP YOUR MARRIAGE ROLLING

Susan, a family friend in her late forties, stopped in to see me one day. She and her husband, Bill, had two sons and a daughter, all of whom were no longer at home. She was obviously upset. She and Bill have been active in church work all their lives but, "I'm to the point where I just don't know what to pray for!" she burst out. For twenty years Bill had neither smoked nor drunk liquor. He even poured gifts of liquor from various manufacturers' representatives down the drain when he received them at Christmas time. Now, for no reason she could determine, he was suddenly changing his habits.

When asked for an explanation, he said he was through trying to be a virtuous person, a "goody-goody" as he saw himself. He told her he was tired of being constantly expected to perform as an ideal husband. He accused Susan of comparing him to other individuals who were either good men or put on good fronts.

"He told me he didn't think he was capable of love any more, that nothing meant anything to him. When I finally convinced him to go with me to our minister to talk it over, he told the clergyman that people in their forties ought to be mature enough to work out their own problems and that he wanted no advice."

After Bill had had several "all-night-out business trips" and frequently had failed to come home on time for dinner, Susan was ready to call a lawyer. However, at the last moment she had second thoughts and instead confided in a mutual friend who suggested she write Bill a letter explaining how she felt since there seemed to be a complete breakdown in verbal communication. This she did. "It's the only thing that has kept us together," she admitted. "He hasn't written to me yet, only a promise of one, but at least I feel better. He hasn't stayed out all night any more." Although things are not all she desires, Susan is trying to be philosophical. She is sure both she and Bill are going through a "change of life" at the same time. "I guess I need to give him the freedom he needs while at the same time giving him my love, affection, and security," she concluded. Like many middle-age men, Bill needs constant reassurance because of the pressures of today's society. He has refused to have a general health checkup, though Susan urged him to do so. He protested that there was nothing a doctor could do for him, despite the fact that after intercourse, which was about once a week, he got severe headaches.

Still hoping to find more answers to her problems, Susan asked if there was a book I could recommend. I suggested *The Intimate Marriage* by Howard J. and Charlotte H. Clinebell. Another suggestion was that she write to the American Association of Marriage Counselors for the name of a competent adviser in her community. Consulting a person who has the skill to see the problem as a whole and who knows the necessary degree of therapy is far better than confiding the problem to a friend, however well-meaning that friend may be. I have been aware of all too many cases when the "best friend" either turned out to have a loose tongue or offered imprudent advice, and as a result the whole matter became a subject of gossip or irrevocable, disastrous decisions were made.

As might be inferred, the big, unanswered question in Susan's mind was "Why?" Why should a perfectly good husband suddenly act so peculiarly? Why do one out of five marriages in middle age end in divorce and many others settle for a dreary compromise? What are the friction points to watch for?

MID-MARRIAGE SLOWDOWN

After twenty-five or more years of marriage, don't be surprised if you awake one morning and get the feeling that the person next to you whom you thought you knew so well is a stranger. Mid-marriage changes hit unexpectedly after the kids have left home. Instead of a growth in understanding, adjustment, and responsiveness to each other's needs, there is a cooling off. The inner growth of strength and mutual love that should continue into old age has been stymied. The zest is gone. One day the couple awakens and finds that, as the cartoon puts it, "It's a new year and the kids have left home." The days have slipped by and even when things seem to be going our way, we wonder what we will do now. What lies ahead?

It is at this vulnerable point that a husband and wife can drift apart and are potential victims of a flirtatious glance at a company Christmas party or a neighborhood gathering, and an innocent kiss can begin a cascade down the chute into infidelity. The change seems sudden but this is not so. The husband and wife have been gradually changing for some time.

Take the experience of Jim, a layman who worked in the denominational headquarters of one of the country's largest churches. He started his job with the intent to do well and through the years had attended many meetings of church groups throughout the country. Now he was in his early fifties, had been married for thirty years, and had just "married off" his youngest daughter. His relations with his wife had become commonplace, unexciting but without many outward signs of friction.

At one of the meetings in the Midwest, he welcomed with a kiss a woman who served on a board of directors of a particular group. Everyone else was greeting with a kiss so he thought nothing about it at first. But for some reason this particular kiss jolted him. Her lips, her perfume, the feeling of warmth in the encounter made him feel good. He had been somewhat restless in his marriage of late but had no desire to get out of it, so this meeting merely left the thought of a pleasant memory. In due time, he found himself enjoying the companionship of the woman at private luncheons when he was in town.

Nothing came of the incident, but he had the feeling that something *could* have happened.

As time went on, he found himself eyeing the pretty girls in the cafeteria. He became an enthusiastic "girl watcher," especially of the "liberated" girls just across the street from where he worked. He was obviously appreciative of the presence of the girls in the office.

Unknowing, Jim's wife teased him about his being in contact with so many good-looking women. He laughed it off, all the while uneasily realizing that he had mentally seduced a number of girls. Actually he never meant to go that far because he loved his wife, but the guilt feelings which resulted made him irritable and moody at home. His wife wondered what had gotten into him.

THE GREEN-EYED MONSTER

A judge in the Domestic Relations Court of Toledo, Ohio, tells the story of a businessman who hired a beautiful and talented secretary. One day his wife happened to visit the office, saw the secretary, and began to worry. Soon after this, the man had to travel to New York to close a big contract, and he took the secretary along to help him. Unable to control her jealousy, his wife began to nag about all sorts of things, and the nagging continued until the secretary eloped with an army captain. A new secretary, capable and efficient but offering no competition to the wife, was hired. Emotional security returned, and his wife stopped her badgering.[1]

Jealousy, combined with nagging, can have the very effect the wife does not want. Trying to get away from such unpleasantness, a man can be attracted to a woman who soothes rather than upbraids. The "other woman" may be escaping from a problem of her own, and the whole matter can become a catastrophe. Marriage should

---

[1] George A. Kelly, *The Catholic Marriage Manual* (New York: Random House, 1958), p. 90.

not be a prison, for when it becomes so, love walks out. Most psychiatrists regard jealousy and possessiveness as a form of sickness.

Insecurity and the doubt of one's hold on the affections of his mate lead to jealousy, and jealousy leads to accusations, whether deserved or not. Complete trust and confidence enables a man or woman to accept the fact that a wife or husband may indulge in a mild flirtation, with no harm done. To individuals in middle age this may merely be a form of convincing one's self that his youth is not too far gone. The difficulty arises, of course, if the mate is not able to accept such actions in the way they are meant. Occasionally we find individuals who purposely seek to cause jealousy so as to reassure themselves that they are still "desirable" and are not really so old after all. While furnishing the plot of many television situation comedies, this is a dangerous game to play in real life.

PERSONALITY CHANGES

We must face the fact that middle age does indeed bring with it certain changes in face, figure, and responsibilities—but when the basic personality changes, we need to look deeper for the causes. For example, if a man or woman has always been meticulous about his or her personal grooming, then over a short period of time "lets himself go," a problem is brewing. In the days of courtship a young man and woman (now in middle age) were more than likely meticulous about their appearance, and after the marriage there were some new things to get used to—curlers, bottles of lotion, creams, five o'clock shadow, more casual dress. After the honeymoon, the marriage might have lost some of its charm, glamor, and romance. But by the time middle age rolls around, a special effort needs to be made to maintain a high standard of personal hygiene and dress. Familiarity should not breed contempt, but on the other hand, neither should it breed carelessness. There is every likelihood that the husband and wife will now have more opportunities to go places together, perhaps even on business trips, and each should be able to feel a pride in the other's appearance.

Closely tied in with personal habits are those involving housekeeping. A marriage will not fail merely because of the way a house looks, of course. Some men want to feel comfortable in a "lived in" atmosphere, while others like to see everything in order. Some women have always maintained a carefree attitude toward housework; others are fastidious. Some men are more than willing to help straighten things up and do the cleaning; others feel it is "woman's work." Be that as it may, when the husband and wife no longer have the children around the house is no time to change housekeeping patterns completely. For example, in one of my early pastorates, a couple felt themselves facing a crisis which, they feared, might lead to bigger problems. Bill suddenly began making a fetish of order in the house. One day he was so angered at seeing sundry items lying about that he hurled them all out on the front lawn. Sandra, his wife, felt both humiliated and angry. In retaliation, she went outside, piled the items belonging to him in one pile and left them there, bringing her own possessions inside. Bill got the message since his pile was quite large, but the incident did nothing to lessen the tension between them, because his basic problem was the dissatisfaction he felt with his job. If feasible, Bill should have left his job or at least should have tried to change some of the more unpleasant aspects of it. He did not, and the bigger problems he and Sandra had foreseen did arise. Bill lacked the fortitude of an executive who hated indoor work, quit his job, found a job where he could work outside, and became a new man, though at half his previous salary.

Similar to Bill's case, a woman just as suddenly began insisting on a certain place for each item, becoming upset if so much as a pillow was moved. She embarrassed her husband by constantly picking up after guests and refusing to serve refreshments in the living room, lest something be spilled. This change indicated something was wrong. Her frustrations were so unformed in her own mind that she could not communicate with anyone. Feeling left out of her husband's busy life and fearful of being rejected or finding herself a failure in the outside world, she had made a fetish of keeping her home immaculate. Anything out of its normal position vaguely alarmed her so she went to all lengths to maintain the status quo.

A woman who has always been reasonably neat about her housekeeping is sending out a signal when she changes, letting dust collect under the bed, in corners and on the stairs, allowing clothing to lie about on chairs for days on end, piling mail, books, magazines, and sundry small objects on any flat surface. Her attitude becomes "What's the use?"

An interesting study reported to the American Association for the Advancement of Science found that wives usually expressed their true feelings about their husbands by the kinds of meals they served. The survey pointed out that the wife who resents her mate will serve him overdone vegetables, meat that is either too rare or burned and no dessert or one that takes little time to prepare.[2] Let me hasten to add that a man should not become perturbed about the next burnt offering that comes his way, for accidents can happen to anyone; however, a persistent indifference indicates that a wife is unhappy over something.

Corey, a minister in his late fifties, recently told me of his own experience. "I found out that this indifference does have a bearing on the marriage. I used to make a good many house calls in the afternoon, and sometimes I just could not get away from the dear little old lady who had to show me, for the tenth time, the pictures of her entire family. Sometimes, I admit, I did not try very hard to get home at the customary dinner hour, figuring that Elaine would manage to have a good dinner ready when-

[2] Ibid., p. 95.

ever I arrived. One evening I was surprised to find two hard and leathery hamburgers on my plate, mushy vegetables in a pan and an apple for dessert. The table was set for one, and I had to eat alone. After that I made every effort to effect some changes in my timing to eliminate the beginning of a real problem. While the kids had been home, I had always made it a point to eat with the family, but after they left I had become careless and took Elaine for granted."

If a wife has an outside job and her time at home is limited, this fact must be taken into consideration. When both partners work, easy-to-prepare meals do not necessarily mean that the wife does not love her husband. I might add that this is definitely not the time for a husband to reminisce about the meals his mother, who spent a great deal of time in the kitchen, prepared. Times have changed and our expectations must change too. However, there is a difference between meals prepared hastily but with love and imagination and those prepared with indifference or carelessness.

Consideration and love are still magic ingredients in marriage, even after many years have passed. A sloppy home and inferior meals often reflect the problems behind them. If a husband finds conditions intolerable, he may depart for haunts more congenial to his taste. Likewise, a wife who is shown little appreciation and affection from her husband may turn elsewhere for solace.

To help develop an empathy for each other, it might be a good idea to exchange places, even for a short time. An executive whose wife was in the hospital for several weeks admitted to me that he had no idea of what went into the managing of a house until he had been forced to try it. "I was surprised to find out what my wife had to put up with day in and day out. The first time I had to do the shopping alone, wash the clothes, do the dishes, and clean the house I realized what she was up against." A wife who has never had to face the world outside the home might consider taking a job, even if for a short period of time, to understand the exhaustion and sometimes tension her husband feels daily.

SEXUAL RELATIONS COOL

"Sexual maladjustment," which we deal with more fully in another chapter, is a sophisticated phrase for the tensions and frustrations that exist in another area of domestic life. As we have pointed out, intimacy once shared sometimes begins to wane in middle age. The wife can become so unresponsive that the husband feels he is losing his sexual vitality and appeal. A woman might hide her emotions on the surface, but her true feelings can make sexual relations difficult or unsatisfying. A vicious circle begins to form in which both husband and wife feel trapped. The more desperately they struggle, the tighter the tensions become, and the situation worsens.

BOREDOM VS. VIM AND VIGOR

Millard Bienvenu, Sr., professor of special education at the University of Southwestern Louisiana, warns that a middle-age couple should be on guard against boredom in their marriage. Some degree of monotony is inevitable because of habit and routine. We might all be bored with our mate at one time or another, but when it happens too frequently and goes too far, this boredom can lead to a breakdown in the marriage. The end result could be for one or the other to reach outside the home for a love affair in an attempt to magically restore youthful romance and excitement.

A new plateau has been reached in the middle years. Change should be countered with change—a new outlook, new habits, new concepts in love making. This may involve enjoying a hobby together, learning and participating in a new sport, or going to a movie, dinner, or weekend away from home together as often as possible.

Lon Ritchie, a television entertainer, says that his favorite story is about the jealous husband who was so sure his wife had a lover that he hired a detective to shadow her and take pictures of what he saw. A few weeks later the detective reported his findings. "Well, here it is," he said. "All the evidence—and with your best friend, too!" He ran the film and the husband saw the pictures of his wife and his best friend as they ate luncheon, took a swim, bowled, danced, and had a fine time. After a while the husband shook his head and said, "I can't believe it; I just can't believe it."

"But," replied the private eye, "the evidence is all here."

"No," answered the confused husband, "that's not what I mean. I just can't believe my wife would be that much fun."

Bob Goddard, writing in the *St. Louis Globe Democrat*, quoted one wife as saying to another, "Reincarnation? Dear me, no. My husband doesn't even believe in life after dinner."

Because we are middle aged does not mean we are past the age of fun. We can discover this as soon as we break out of the stultifying, programed way of living we find ourselves in and return to being our true selves.

The woman riding the exercise cycle has the right idea as she says to her husband, also on a cycle, "Honey, why don't we ever go anywhere?"

To get away from the bogged down feeling of not getting anywhere, the Rev. William H. Genne, a member of the staff of the National Council of Churches department of family life and a prominent United Church of Christ lecturer on family and marriage, says that couples can inject excitement and new life into their marriages by undergoing a joint stocktaking, changing their spending, vacation, and work habits.

A minister who realized that he needed to combat boredom resigned from his large suburban church and purchased a home on the Atlantic coast in Georgia. Now he and his wife go for long walks every morning and evening along the ocean. He supports them both by writing and giving a limited number of lectures. This couple has come to regard the mature years as the payoff on an investment of many years together, many problems shared, children raised and sent out into the world, and countless exchanged expressions of love.

If you're in a rut, get out. Ruts are dangerous!

WHAT CAN YOU DO?

To discover ways to make a marriage in the middle years more flexible, happy, and enduring is not easy unless you've been working at it all along. Anything worthwhile requires and demands effort. But there is hope and with it does come joy. These suggestions might help to alleviate some of the sources of friction which arise from time to time.

• Watch for small areas of friction and try to get rid of them before they become overwhelming. In my own married life, I have been plagued with an insignificant problem in the bathroom: my family has persisted in squeezing the toothpaste from the top of the tube so that after a few mornings the top looks like a crushed fender and the bottom swells like a sausage ready to explode. While the kids were at home, I could tolerate the condition, occasionally lecturing them on the advantages of squeezing from the bottom. I would painstakingly re-form the tube and eventually even bought small keys to wrap the tube up from the bottom. But now I've learned that my wife, Margie, continues this annoying habit. But she resents criticism of it because she feels she should not be lectured like a child. I do not know what a psychologist would say about such a situation, but there it is. It remains as annoying as her dropping tissues all over the house, yard, and car during the hay fever season.

On the other side of the fence, I like to lightly pinch or jab Margie on the arm as a show of affection. She hates this practice, however, because she bruises easily and even a slight pinch results in a black and blue mark.

Such insignificant sources of irritation can be symptoms of a deeper malady. When the dust settles, a couple might be able to say to each other, "What you really are telling me is that you don't care enough to stop doing things that you know very well make me angry and frustrated." It is the feeling of a lack of concern with our difficulties that brings about those flares in temper.

It might be that an overlooked signal for a romantic experience has led to such outward expressions as the arm jab, tissue dropping, failure to move the seat back in the car (especially irritating when the husband has long legs which are pushed up under his chin), feeding the dog before feeding the husband, reading the paper or magazine while the wife is talking, or failing to match socks carefully before putting them in the drawer. On the other hand, it might merely be a result of taking each other too much for granted that has led to the lack of consideration or thoughtlessness.

As an exercise (*which won't work unless both are completely honest with each other*), *the husband should make a list of the things he knows he does which irritate his wife, and the wife should list the things she knows she does which disturb her husband. Then these lists should be verbalized frankly.* No one is accusing anyone of anything, but irritations are brought into the open. Understanding reached on small issues can open doors to future talks and a closer intimacy.

• Spruce up your appearance. Keep your clothing clean and neat even when the time is to be spent at home in the company of the husband or wife alone. Good grooming shows you care what your spouse thinks of you.

• Recharge your batteries by getting away together. This may mean a weekend trip, a vacation spent in surroundings appealing to both parties, or even an afternoon or evening at a movie or sports event. Margie and I enjoy high school football games, so we break a fairly heavy schedule and go nearly every Saturday. We go into the city for dinner and a show occasionally, when we feel we can afford it. There are many things a couple can do together. *Make a list of places you mutually like to go or the*

things you both like to do and plan to try one of them every Friday or Saturday night for a month.
- Learn to control your hostile impulses. The late William C. Menninger, president of the Menninger Foundation, says that all of us are born with hostile feelings and impulses. If we recognize that they exist, we can learn to handle them in constructive ways. Frequently our spouse becomes the innocent victim of our negative emotions. Shunning responsibility, running out on a situation, neglecting those we love, carrying out thoughtless actions, rejecting what we once held dear, demonstrating unfaithfulness, or simply being completely forgetful can be manifestations of these hidden emotions.

Jealousy afflicts people in varying degrees, and must be controlled. The recognition that jealousy stems from some form of insecurity should help us understand it. Most men and women, especially in middle age, feel a degree of satisfaction when their mates still attract an admiring eye—if they have trust in each other. If they are mutually secure, jealousy need not result. Both men and women should keep in mind the motto, "When a man stops looking, he is dead."
- Don't expect perfection, even after all these years together. No one can lay claim to perfection.
- Think affirmatively to build up day-to-day energy. A continual negative feeling can end in a morass of despair. *As an exercise, read Psalm 73 and analyze it. Why did the psalmist feel depressed? What did he do to lift himself out of this negativism?* He went to the "sanctuary" and straightened out his own thinking, learning that the world wasn't at fault. He was. Sometimes the ego needs a bit of self-examination.
- Change your pace. Encourage friendship. Ride your hobby. Find new diversions that bring out your hidden energy and discover how exciting and absorbing interests spark a sagging complex.
- Show appreciation. It is the best way to eliminate friction and fan the flame in your mate's heart.

5 COPING WITH A CRISIS

> I am a man in my middle years and I've had an active, relatively happy sex life. Suddenly, I've been very worried because I find I'm impotent with my wife. I was so concerned about this that I had several extramarital relations and found that I had no problem with these women.
>
> Actually, I got quite a charge out of the fact that I was doing something that, for me, was unusual and I suppose I felt guilty about that. Both of these brief relationships have given me more pleasure than I have experienced in a long time. Now I'm a bit confused and not sure where to go next. H.H.[1]

This letter, which appeared in one of New Jersey's newspapers, is related by a nationally known, syndicated columnist. Keep it in mind, for I'll comment on it later. Here is another one.

> My husband is a wonderful provider, a good man, not a philanderer. His one bad habit is that he flatters every woman he meets. He bolsters their ego at the expense of mine, i.e., "I'd give anything if my wife baked bread like this!" or "You're as young looking as when you were in college with us."
>
> If I retaliate by giving a man friend a compliment, my husband implies I'm stuck on him. Considering the terrible problems I read in your column, mine seems slight, but . . . I can't stand the sly glances women give me when he's slathering on the praise. Dorothy.[2]

[1] Joyce Brothers, "Wife's Attitude Can Be Cause of Impotence," *The Star Ledger*, Newark, N.J. (Sept. 24, 1971), p. 29.
[2] Helen Bottel, "Helen Help Us," *The Star Ledger*, Newark, N.J. (Oct. 3, 1971), p. 6.

That letter also appeared in the newspaper in a nationally syndicated column. Here is still another, addressed to one of the best known of the advice columnists.

> My husband and I have been married for forty long, boring, miserable, rotten years. I don't know how a woman of my intelligence and refinement could have chosen such a coarse, vulgar man. All these years we have existed under the same roof, although we have nothing in common. He loves dirty jokes, hunting and fishing, and plenty of sex. I am soft spoken, cultured and genteel. Next year the slob retires, and the thought of having him at home under my feet all day gives me a sick feeling at the pit of my stomach. I want to do some traveling with people of my own class. We are financially able to take some lovely trips, but he'd rather hunt and fish with his lowbrow friends. I am still attractive and could enjoy the companionship of a high-type man. Would a divorce at age sixty-two be such a terrible thing? A Real Lady.[3]

As we read these three requests for advice, we find several situations. In the first illustration, the husband obviously is having a sexual problem with his wife and this, in turn, has involved other women. In our second letter, the husband has bad manners and degrades his wife in public. Underlying this problem could be several more serious issues, one of which might be a marriage that is best described as "blah." He's a nice guy, but he finds satisfaction in complimenting women other than his wife. The possibility exists that he eventually might find himself in an extra-marital relationship. In our third letter, it is apparent that the wife has an extremely low opinion of her husband, which has evidently developed over many years.

As I peruse magazines, books and newspapers, I am continually amazed at the variety of intricate, sometimes

---

[3] From the book, *Ann Landers Says Truth Is Stranger . . .* by Ann Landers, pp. 174–75. © 1968 by Ann Landers. Reprinted with permission of the publishers, Prentice-Hall, Inc., Englewood Cliffs, New Jersey.

almost ridiculous, problems of marriage that individuals face in middle age.

UNEMPLOYMENT AS A MARRIAGE FACTOR

Whenever I am in various groups, I learn that certain acquaintances are faced with unemployment or the imminent prospect of unemployment. For example, when two corporations merged recently, a man in his early fifties suddenly found himself adrift because his job was consolidated with another and a younger man was retained to head the department. Anyone who has faced this situation or has read of similar ones in various national magazines knows that at fifty, jobs are not easy to come by, even though a man can yet look forward to a great many years of productive output. Automation and computerization are making some skills obsolescent and there are no others to take their place.

Unemployment, whatever the cause, can lead to all kinds of problems at home. It may mean drawing on savings put aside for retirement, accepting a lesser paying job or one of lesser importance, cutting back on living standards, or the wife's getting a job outside the home. All involve adjustments that may or may not cause a rift in the marriage, depending on the individuals. If the husband continues to look for work but is unsuccessful, his morale is at a dangerous low. Much depends on the love, understanding, and confidence between husband and wife as to what the long-term effects of the unemployment will be. If he is married to a woman who equates wage earning with masculinity, he might find himself involved in a series of destructive patterns. His wife might become "motherly" while he could respond with a false bravado which he cannot maintain.

FINANCES

Unemployment leads to another strain on marriage: money problems, sometimes more of a symptom than a cause of conflict. Conflicts in role concepts, ego clashes, or just plain lack of know-how can be basic causes. Lack of knowledge can be remedied fairly easily if the desire to do so is present but the other conflicts need careful advice.

A woman who had been married for twenty-two years to a husband who earned $40,000 a year was having a serious financial problem of her own. He handled all the money and refused to give her an allowance. His reasoning was, "Why? You are home all day. I'll pay all the bills and you won't have to worry about them." The only time she could get any money from him was when he was in a romantic mood and this precipitated all kinds of ego problems for her, reducing her concept of herself to that of a prostitute. She had read in a newspaper column that "when sex is used by a wife as a payment for favors and is withheld for punishment, it places the marriage at the level of prostitution."

As the use of credit cards has increased, so has the number of traps which can damage a marriage. All too many people fall victim to impulse buying and fail to control their desires, though they recognize their foolishness when the bills come in. Look around at magazines, television, and newspapers—all of them by sight and sound are geared to induce buying. Business and industry have employed the best psychologists to persuade us to buy items we may or may not need, usually the latter.

Door-to-door salesmen fall into the same category as the media in this respect. An event that occurred in the early years of our marriage served one good purpose, although it made me unhappy at the time. I have become highly suspicious of bargains and I can't afford "pressure" salesmanship, especially when I am told that I must make up my mind immediately or the opportunity will be gone forever.

One evening I received a telephone call from an encyclopedia salesman. He had an offer which we would be sure to find attractive. I tried to forestall him, but, alas, I was no match for his persuasiveness. He arrived the next afternoon when both my wife and I were at home. At the time I was earning $2,000 a year (not much even in those days) in my first pastorate, and we had one child, an eighteen-month-old son. The salesman gave his pitch. He made it sound attractive: small monthly payments, lists of satisfied customers, some of whom I recognized as former seminary classmates of mine, the information that ours was a *special* family to whom this great bargain could be given, and (this was the clincher) we could not possibly educate this eighteen-month-old child without a set of the encyclopedia in the house. We had to make up our minds that night; there would be no thinking about it for a few days or talking it over with other people.

To make a long story short, we succumbed to the inducements and signed the agreement to pay ten dollars down (which the salesman "generously" loaned us from his own pocket, since we did not have that much in the house) and to pay ten dollars every month for eighteen months. Believe me, those monthly payments were a source of irritation and deprivation for us.

Unforeseen money problems can throw a marriage off the track unless there is some plan to enable the couple to meet them. As retirement looms, there is a real possibility that couples will live in resentful misery because there was little or no planning for the time of less economic productivity.

MILES APART

Temporary separation because of job transfers to other areas or countries can strain a marriage and reawaken fears of abandonment, rejection, and loss of love. Many preparations need to be made, the house sold, farewells made to close friends, personal commitments discontinued. If the wife has held a job she enjoys, she may not really want to give it up. Occasionally, a commuting marriage is the result.

In these times of separation, there is loneliness to contend with. When I left Blue Island, Illinois, to move to New Jersey, I had to leave the family behind for six months. Having no one close to share the events of the day, the doubts, or the triumphs, was a lonely feeling. Planning the bridges over the separation and looking forward to pleasures to come help avoid psychological pitfalls.

IN SICKNESS AND IN HEALTH

In illness the emotional balance of a family can be sent reeling. The woman is not only filled with anxiety about her husband's health but she also may have to consider the temporary loss of financial support and the shouldering of family problems. If the wife is sick, the husband has to fulfill several roles: housekeeper, cook, shopper, launderer. Resentments, perhaps subconscious, can form over the prolonged necessity of doing double duty. We can sympathize with the coach who wondered about his injured quarterback: "Will he ever be able to take over his responsibilities again?"

Sickness in other branches of the family can take its toll if it means extra time spent away from home, large medical expenses, increased emotional upsets, and the like. Frank discussion is needed to set guidelines for such situations.

DEAR MOM AND DAD

The responsibility of caring for aging parents can be a source of tension. In some cases it is necessary for the parent to move in with the family. This can work out beautifully, yet it frequently seems to create difficulties. Some couples have added a room and bath to ensure privacy for their parents. But what happens when a long, debilitating illness strikes? What about the problems created by brothers and sisters who might not think that Mom or Dad is getting a fair shake from the child he is living with? What can be done about the strained relationship created by a wife who loves her mother very much and has invited her to live at her home, only to realize that the husband does not really get along well with his mother-in-law? Life becomes increasingly difficult if circumstances compel him to support the aging parent and curtail his and his wife's social life. Guilt feeling can muddy the tranquil waters. Older parents do not always realize the extra demands they can cause in a household, and, of course, there is the chance that an older person can feel unwanted and unloved.

TARRYING LONG AT THE WINE
Liquor, with its financial and personality problems, is one of the biggest causes of marital conflict. Some counselors list it as the most serious cause of divorce; 60 percent of divorces are caused by alcohol.

Irene was lonely, and she had a drinking problem. When she and her husband were invited out by friends, she would take one cocktail and get into an argument, saying insulting things to her friends. After two drinks she passed out. Irene recognized her problem and swore she would never drink again, only to find herself potted at the next party. What could she do? What should her husband, both embarrassed and worried, do about it?

SEPARATION BY DEATH
Another problem that can befall a couple in the middle years is the death of one of the partners. In one case, a man's wife of thirty-five years died, and he took the separation hard, going into complete seclusion for several months. In most cases, death is a shattering experience, leaving its mark for a long, long period. The passage of time does help the grief, but healing involves the open acknowledgment of the emotions caused by the loss. Kept within, fear, self-accusations, and self-punishment begin to fester. Released, they can act as a purgative. But how are we to draw the line between this release and becoming maudlin and tiresome to friends?

Recently there has been more and more concern with death. Even high school young people become preoccupied with it, and many of their creative pieces of writing deal with the subject. When a course on death was offered at New York University, the interest was so high that many students had to be turned away. Yet when an audience in its middle years is confronted with the subject, they can't take it. One can talk about love, hate, sex, or war—but not death. Even in obituaries the phrase "he died" is dispensed with in favor of "he passed away" or "he departed this life." Why can't so many middle-age people face the inevitability of death?

In the foregoing pages I have pointed out problems of marriages as they apply particularly to middle age. You can add more, some that are major ones, while others are relatively minor yet have assumed unusual proportions. Some difficulties may be adjusted by dialogue, give-and-take, and listening. Others will require more drastic measures.

DOUBTFUL ADVICE

There are many individuals who simply do not know where to turn in times of crisis. It is difficult to find just the person we want to talk to, one who will listen and not gossip. Often problems involve enough shame so that it seems easier to write about them rather than to talk about them. And some individuals can express themselves more lucidly through the written word rather than speech.

Troubled souls who are ready to bare their private problems in public to newspaper and magazine counselors number in the thousands. Some of us may recall Dorothy Dix, said to have received five hundred letters a day for her advice on love and domestic problems. These were syndicated in 150 newspapers with a daily circulation of twenty million. We may remember Beatrice Fairfax as well. She claimed that in ten years she had received a million letters. The newspapers called her the nation's preeminent counselor on social decorum and personal problems. She became a kind of Delphic oracle whose opinions were sought in as many as eight hundred letters a day.

Today we have a new breed of magazine and newspaper counselor, represented by such popular columnists as Ann Landers who "speaks out on family battles, marriage, money, and sex." Ann Landers says she spends ten to twelve hours daily answering thousands of letters from all over the world. Today her syndicated column appears in more than seven hundred newspapers around the world with a readership of fifty-four million.

Fortunately, Miss Landers falls back on professional help in answer to many of the problems that come to her. And she admits that she cannot solve problems; each individual must solve his own. She sees her main purpose as a "catalyst . . . an unbiased observer . . . to offer an ear or shoulder to cry on." Her correspondents state frequently that they need someone "who will listen, and there isn't anyone else."

In the cases cited at the beginning of this chapter, the individuals had turned to newspaper columnists for advice. Ordinarily, one would feel that Joyce Brothers, who answered H.H., would give him sound advice since she is trained in the field. However, without knowing (at least from the printed letter) the details of the married life of H.H. or anything about his wife, Dr. Brothers violates one of the rules of current therapy practice whereby she "sees only one spouse." Today a therapist insists on seeing both husband and wife so that their habitual patterns of interaction can be directly observed.

Dr. Brothers advises H.H., "From your letter I would assume that you are going through some sort of stress with your wife which is producing the feeling of anxiety and resulting impotence. This may be brought on by your wife, either consciously or unconsciously. . . . It seems to me that much of your problem may actually rest with your wife's attitudes."

Anyone who has listened to couples with marriage problems knows that both want allies. If they appear individually before a minister, lawyer, or counselor, there is a recitation, a litany and accusation of the faults of the mate. Not knowing the other spouse, the therapist is in no position to question or challenge the statements. So we can only imagine what has been done to H.H.'s ego when he is told that "your problem rests with your wife's attitudes." What about the wife? How are her attitudes to be discussed or changed? How about H.H.'s attitudes?

The popular "marriage columnists" are more than likely very sincere in trying to help the individuals who write to them. Some advisers, such as David Reuben, are experts in the field. Nevertheless, they can only speak on issues in general terms. In a recent popular feature, "Sex and Middle Age," Dr. Reuben makes some excellent prognostications. Still each person is unique, and each problem must be considered on its individual merits. Many more facts need to be studied about the couple wrestling with their middle-age sex problems.

The advice found in books, magazines, and newspapers can be worthwhile as a source of information that should spur us on to seek more personal help. So it is with this book. You will, hopefully, find a great deal of information that relates to your living. Some of your problems you will solve by using common sense or by getting a new perspective, but if the difficulty is complex, writing to an advice columnist or reading a book will not provide the answers.

Occasionally, advice given can cause havoc in the lives of others. For example, a newspaper counselor printed a letter received from a man seriously crippled with arthritis. To support the two of them, his wife had had to take a job. After a time, she fell in love with a wealthy businessman, went to live with him, and now sought a divorce from her husband. She had promised the invalid money and a room in a retirement center. But even if he refused the divorce, she told him, she would continue to live with her lover because she felt she truly loved him more than life itself. The distraught husband wanted to know what to do.

The forthcoming advice was the type that often becomes a *fata morgana,* luring marriages onto the reefs. The columnist said that the husband must remember that life was hard on his wife in nursing a sick man. She actually would have had to spend her life in "slavery" rather than enjoying the ease, comfort, soft living, and freedom from financial worry. The advice was that although it seemed heartless for her to leave, it was her happiness against that of her husband, and therefore a divorce should be granted so that the wife's position could be legalized. Thus, claimed the columnist, the husband would avoid the feeling of petty revenge and "you will have made the gallant gesture of a fine gentleman."

After reading this answer, a person could feel that the props or buttresses which the church and society had given to marriage were being pulled out. The easy, attention-getting, clever answer to a serious problem affecting human lives is a false one.

FATE IN THE STARS?

In this "Age of Aquarius" there are more and more individuals looking to astrology for advice on varieties of subjects. One newspaper item attests to this. In San Jose, California, after twenty-eight years of married life, a husband read in an astrology book that he and his wife were born under adverse planets. He requested that his wife file suit for divorce so that he might find a mate that had been born under a more congenial planet. She acquiesced, for by this time she had learned that her husband was obsessed with the power of the stars.

Most of the advice sought from astrologers is related to home life and family relations. In an interview with a "seer" who advertised in a daily paper, she brought out that individuals that consulted her wanted to know the following: Does she (he) love me? Is she (he) true to me? Where was she (he) last night? Have I met the right mate? How can I hold my wife (husband) or, conversely, How can I get rid of her (him)?

In a study made a few years ago, it was found that four out of every ten people believed in some kind of fortune telling. As long ago as forty years, *The New York Times* reported that

> Fortune tellers and their kind break up more homes in the United States than any other one cause. People go to such persons to get answers to only two questions—questions of love and money. Fortune tellers have found that plain, matter-of-fact answers do not interest their clients, so they tell them their wife or husband is interested in some other person and thus sow the seeds of jealousy.[4]

A GOOD FRIEND IS NOT SO GOOD

As mentioned earlier, a "good friend" is not the person to turn to for effective advice and counsel on marriage. A woman of my acquaintance has been experiencing marital problems which probably could have been worked out with competent help. But to whom has she turned for advice? To a neighbor, a well-meaning and sympathetic neighbor who is long on advice but also, unfortunately, possessed of a wagging tongue. That trusted neighbor has informed the entire neighborhood of her "friend's problems," in a sympathetic way, of course, until those problems have been compounded and real trouble lies ahead.

I hear men asking other men for personal advice as they ride the commuter train going to and from work each day. The advice runs the gamut from thoughtful to ridiculous, but I personally wonder just what would happen in those homes if even half of this freely given counsel were heeded.

Parents and in-laws on both sides of the family also

---

[4] *The New York Times* (July 14, 1931). © 1931 by The New York Times Company. Reprinted by permission.

come under the classification of poor advice-givers. Since they are emotionally involved themselves, their ideas are seldom objective, and even more alienation can result.

THE ENCOUNTER GROUPS

How about sensitivity groups, that new "therapy" which has been discussed so frequently of late? Mobile and lonely, comfortably well off and frustrated, millions of Americans have turned to encounter groups as a way to explore self-understanding, a way to practice relating more deeply to other persons. In such groups the main focus is taken away from the emphasis on individual counseling and psychotherapy and stresses the group. Some individuals still regard encounter groups as a part of a Communist plot while others, hearing about the sensationalism which has resulted from a few so-called "nude marathons," condemn the whole idea.

There is no doubt that many couples have found encounter groups a way in which the marital relationship can be helped. Changes in attitudes and behavior, emotional, intellectual, and physical well-being have taken place. The feedback from one person to another lets the individual learn how he appears to others and what impact he has in interpersonal relationships. As a result, there is improved communication, new ideas, and new directions emerging for marriages. What is a hoped for result is that the individual comes from behind his façade to relate better to others and the life situations he faces.

What has drawn people to this movement? Carl Rogers, the dean of the encounter group movement, feels that it is a hunger for something that the person does not find in his work, church, and family life. He writes:

> It is a hunger for relationships which are close and real; in which feelings and emotions can be spontaneously expressed without first being carefully censored or bottled up, where deep experiences—disappointments and joys—can be

shared, where new ways of behaving can be risked and tried out, where, in a word, he approaches the state where all is known and accepted, and thus further growth becomes possible. This seems to be the overpowering hunger which he hopes to satisfy through his experiences in an encounter group.[5]

Not everyone is in favor of the encounter group as a source of help for problems. Many orthodox psychologists and psychiatrists have frowned on the development. There are risks involved such as a person becoming so involved in revealing himself that he is left with serious problems that are not worked through. He becomes so disturbed by psychotic episodes that he must go to a therapist for help in straightening things out.

There is also a great danger to marriage when only one of the couple has attended an encounter group session. During an experience, a person can change so much that the husband or wife is at a loss to understand what has taken place. One of the frequent aftereffects of intensive group experience is that it brings out into the open for discussion marital tensions which have been kept under cover. Therefore someone must be ready and able to help cope with the dilemmas raised.

There is a positive, warm, and loving feeling that can develop between members of encounter groups which, when understood in the context of the group, causes no difficulty. When, however, the marriage partner has not been present, he may interpret this feeling incorrectly and feel that his mate is slipping away, regardless of the facts in the case.

One husband who had attended one of the meetings told me about his experience with Ruth, a member of the group. He had developed a very warm feeling for Ruth, a compassion, because he felt she was lonely. She lived in a

---

[5] Carl Rogers, *Carl Rogers on Encounter Groups* (New York: Harper & Row, 1970), p. 11.

small town and rarely was able to get away from her duties. After she left the group, she wrote a long, affectionate letter to the man who had befriended her. He, in turn, showed the letter to his wife, pleased that Ruth would confide in him as a friend. His wife, however, was not proud at all. In fact, she was alarmed because she read a love affair, or a potential one, into the letter. The husband stopped writing to Ruth until his wife, in turn, went to an encounter group and came to understand the involvement of feelings.

Not all episodes end this harmoniously. So I can only say that a person must be very careful in his involvement in group experiences. They do have their value because of the kind of world we live in, but one must also be aware of the faddists, cultists, manipulators, recognition seekers, and even well-meaning but inept leaders of such groups.

WHERE CAN YOU TURN?

I would suggest that you read the latest literature which reflects the experiences of others. There are some excellent books written by competent and trained individuals. Read the advice columnists, but don't let that advice be the final word.

Be big enough to go for outside help to a qualified minister, physician, or trained marriage counselor. In most cases these individuals have had experience in counseling or, if not, can give recommendations as to where to go for further help. Unfortunately, some church members do not have enough confidence in their ministers and would feel uneasy consulting them. I can understand this. I certainly would hesitate to talk to some ministers about personal matters. They may talk too much, usually carelessly, and some have gone so far as to use confidences as illustrations in sermons, thinly disguising the actual circumstances. Frankly, on several occasions when I had a problem I wanted to discuss, I found I could not turn to another minister. I have had the experience of confiding in a person, only to learn that the information had been spread among my acquaintances. Lay men and women may not value the judgments of their minister. I recently heard several families of a church in a neighboring town speak disparagingly with levity bordering on ridicule about their minister. At the time, I asked myself, "Would anyone want to go to ask him for serious advice?"

We are not to be interpreted as indicating that ministers as a whole are not to be trusted with confidential information. There are certainly those in the clergy who can effectively handle emotional and problematic situations. The point being brought out is that one should approach a person in whom he has confidence and whom he knows to be reliable, whether the help is sought from the minister, lawyer, or family physician. A more impersonal marriage counselor might be the answer.

STEPS FOR HANDLING PROBLEMS

We have looked at some of the crises that come to middle-age couples. We have urged caution in choosing those to whom we turn for help. But there are some practical suggestions that you can begin to work on yourself, if both you and your mate really are serious about keeping, or making, yours a rewarding relationship.

1. Start where you are. Take as objective a look as possible (not always easy, I admit) at the situation and examine the problem to get an idea of the direction you should go.

2. Use the resources that you already have. Start with your ideas, the opportunities you have, the physical advantages you possess.

3. Stop looking for magic answers and tricky solutions to problems. There are none. Pain, discomfort, and a degree of unpleasant "facing things as they are" may be necessary in the process.

4. Be willing to ask for help. It is true that Christians can really be "anti-Christian" in their feeling that somehow

they must solve their own problems. The theological word here is "pride." If we get to the place where we confess that we simply do not know what is wrong or what to do next, it is at just that point when competent advice must be sought. Remember, however, that advice or help might not be exactly what you want to hear.

5. Learn from experience. We can find others who have weathered the storms, and we can read about those who have gone through problems as bad or worse than our own. By studying what went wrong, we might see how to improve our own situations.

6. Prepare for a long haul. Some problems are not going to be solved as quickly as we'd like. Adjustment, patience, or even compromise may be needed.

7. A time of crisis is the very time when tender thoughtfulness is a must. Give demonstrations of it in action and in words, even if a degree of role-playing is involved.

8. Prayer is powerful; don't neglect it.

6 LET'S QUARREL CONSTRUCTIVELY

Eugène Ionesco's short scenario of the absurd, *Anger,* portrays a chilling modern parable. On an idyllic Sunday in an idyllic small town all appears to be tranquil. The local beggar is given money and smiles; husbands and wives are kind and courteous to each other. However, after the inhabitants of this Eden go home for lunch, the husbands find flies in their soup. Frowns and cross words result. Insults become more and more virulent. Soup bowls and other crockery are thrown. The police arrive. What began as a domestic then civil disturbance becomes a global war and eventually an atomic holocaust. The final scene, shown on television, is of the planet exploding—because of flies in the soup.

Anger can be dangerous and can lead to untold miseries. Conversely, anger properly understood and channeled can lead to better relationships between husband and wife.

On a television interview, a middle-age couple was asked to describe their marriage. They concurred that never had they had a quarrel or spoken harsh words. The interviewer's only comment was, "Doesn't that make life a little dull?"

Anger and quarrels can play a constructive part in marriage, particularly in marriages of twenty to thirty years. When the children have left home, new situations and life patterns tend to pose new stresses and frustrations. With the one-to-one relationship, these stresses and frustrations need a safety valve which a "healthy" quarrel can provide.

THE DANGER OF UNEXPRESSED ANGER

Today the need for the expression of anger is regarded in psychiatric circles not only as moral but also as something even better: healthy and therapeutic. A fight a day keeps the doctor away suggests psychiatrist Theodore Isaac Rubin in his *The Angry Book*. He asks: "Have you experienced the good, clean feel that comes after expressing anger, as well as the increased self-esteem and the feel of real peace with one's self and others?"

In *The Intimate Enemy*, George R. Bach, a clinical psychologist, turns anger into an art, or possibly a science. "Intimate hostilities," he guarantees, "can be programed." Dr. Bach, like Rubin, has his own slogan: "The family that fights together stays together."[1] If you are not an expert at being angry, the helpful circumstance is that Dr. Bach teaches you how to be angry and do a good job of it. Probably one of our real problems is that, as with so many other things, we botch the opportunities to be angry in a constructive way.

There are several reasons why we have by middle age not learned the refreshing benefits of a nice quarrel. A long and admittedly happily married woman expressed it bluntly. "Every once in a while Bill and I fight like hell. The thing is, I guess, we know how to do it."

First of all, courtship did not prepare us for disagreements and differences of opinion. Prior to marriage, each of the couple tries to bring out his best image. When there are incipient difficulties, the partners-to-be tend to carefully overlook or excuse certain displeasing habits and attitudes. As the years pass, however, these same habits or even once endearing idiosyncrasies take on a different color.

In private conversations with a couple contemplating separation, a husband admitted to having been slightly

---

[1] *Time* (Aug. 16, 1971), p. 40.

annoyed by his then bride-to-be's incessant smoking. Thirty years later, this habit has become a major grievance in their relationship. He says the odor of stale cigarettes drives him out of the house and that she is threatening her own health. She replies that what she does is none of his business and that it's too late for her to change. After all, he hasn't stopped those weekly poker games with the "boys" which put their finances in jeopardy all too often. Never had this couple sat down and brought out their true feelings before. Instead, they had alternately ignored or made snide, sneering remarks about their sources of irritation. The silent tactic that prophesies "After marriage, he (she) will change," meaning of course, "*I'll* change him (her)," does not work.

Couples who have not learned to pepper their marriages with frank disputes are likely to discover that they are harboring unexpressed hostility or resentment, leading to more damage emotionally than an out-and-out quarrel. Over the years, these hidden hostilities can develop into a devastating pattern which can lead to a complete break in relations, especially after the children are no longer there as "buffers." The husband may cultivate an extra-marital affair based on the feeling that "Here is a woman that truly understands me." If he really wants to "fight dirty," he can always allow his wife to know about the affair. The woman may do likewise, or if not so overt in her solution, lead a life completely separate from that of her husband except for the fact that they reside in the same house.

There are other ways these pent-up hostilities may surface. The man may spend an inordinate amount of time at his work, deluding himself into believing that he is indispensable. He may choose to spend his free time away from home with friends of kindred spirits. Still another tactic is treating his wife as if she were a slightly lesser creature (and actually believing it) under the guise of being an overly helpful and understanding husband.

The wife, on the other hand, wages war in her own way. She may play the role of martyr. A few choice statements around the neighborhood and soon everyone is feeling sorry for her. She may turn to nagging, riding her husband after he comes home from work, getting ready to dig the spurs into him on the weekend. It's no wonder then that by Sunday night he is ready to shout, "Get off my goddamn back!"

She may resort to being the depressed, demanding "little girl," the all-wise mother, or the sexually unsatisfied lover. The latter really gets the man. He ends up feeling as if he had been socked in the guts. And, of course, when all else fails, there is the inevitable silent treatment.

This last tactic—silence—on the part of either the husband or the wife can break down communication and corrode a marriage rapidly. As a teenager, I had a good friend who was a Roman Catholic. The parents did not believe in divorce or even separation, so they had already lived together for ten years in complete silence. The only way they communicated was through my friend Joe or his older brother. As I look back on this marriage now, it is obvious that this couple never quarreled. But what kind of a marriage was it?

Sometimes we fear our negative feelings and try to camouflage them. When there are children around, we try to hide our quarrels and anger. Most of us have been raised with the idea that "it is bad to quarrel in front of the children." So a husband and wife may fear what will happen if anger erupts. Each may feel that if he gives vent to his anger, the emotion will overwhelm him and he will lose control. He may fear that his anger will breed anger in return or that he will lose the love of his spouse. Sometimes the floundering situation winds up with the couple joining a group therapy situation where help may or may not be forthcoming. Dr. Bach is under the apprehension that in this new "industry," a cult of anger-fakers could develop which will do more harm than good.

ANGER IS AN ALARM SYSTEM

Once the initial storm has passed, the normal expression of anger *can* lead to deeper sympathy and understanding. One wife said,

> If we do not have the opportunity to quarrel over a problem, I feel as if there is a lid clamped on me while all the time the fire keeps building up the steam. The fight is like an escape valve. When it's all over, I feel closer to my husband; we go into the bedroom and make up, and I feel there is much more of mutual trust between us. We realize that we really do love each other.

The very act of differing gives us a perspective, needed as much in marriages as it is needed by the artist who constantly backs off from his painting to see his work as a whole. If accepted wisely and handled deftly, differences can lead to a better and stronger marriage.

Before giving quarrels carte blanche in marital affairs, we must add a few words of caution. Consider the case of Shirley and Ed, as we shall call them, two people whose marital problems got away from them. One evening Shirley came to my church study to talk to me about her family problems, particularly her relationship with her husband. As her story unfolded, it became obvious that Shirley and Ed needed professional help. But I felt I could at least listen and enable Shirley, and later Ed, to bring their problems into the open, hoping it would alleviate matters.

Their marriage had cooled by the middle years; the intimacy was gone. Among the major problems, according to Shirley, was Ed's constant drinking and his subsequent reactions, especially at parties, which they frequently attended. "He embarrasses me," she confessed. "He begins to paw women after he has had a few drinks. And if I'm nearby, he has a nasty habit of pinching my breasts. If I avoid him, he makes a public issue of it."

These drinking episodes usually led to violent arguments after they had returned home. Sometimes they would begin earlier, in the front seat of the car. Shirley, admitting to taking a drink or two herself, would enter into the shouting match as they drove home. The altercations continued until the early morning hours.

Ed, when I spoke with him later, confirmed that these arguments had occurred with more frequency and vehemence through the years. Now that the children had left for college, Ed and Shirley's home life had deteriorated into vindictive accusations interspersed with frosty silences.

The problems of Shirley and Ed had gone beyond the scope of a concerned pastor, and I finally convinced them to seek professional help. In subsequent conversations, I learned that the marriage was not to be terminated after all, as Shirley had first indicated. However, there was a long way to go and much self-examination by both parties before the wounds could be healed. Nevertheless, I felt progress had been made.

For this reason, I was shocked when Shirley's mother called some months later. Ed and Shirley had gone to a party where a great deal of drinking took place. An argument ensued, with "friends" alternately sympathizing with and castigating the two. On the way home, Ed accused his wife of paying too much attention to a particular bachelor. This led to a rehashing of previous times Ed had felt Shirley was the center of the attention of men at the party. Shirley retaliated by calling Ed a "lush" and a "drunk," telling him he was a "dirty old man" who made passes at anything in skirts. But the altercation did not end there. After dropping Shirley at home, Ed drove off recklessly in a state of drunken anger, and, encountering the bachelor from the evening's party outside a local bar, proceeded to pump six bullets into his wife's "suitor."

Shirley obtained a divorce, and Ed is still serving time for murder, a tragic end to a marriage. What evolved here has led experts such as Rebecca Liswood, a practicing physician who has had some extensive training in marital and pre-marital counseling to suggest some "don'ts" regarding quarreling between husbands and wives.[2]

WATCH OUT!

1. Don't quarrel when you have been drinking. In such instances you are likely to say things that you really did not intend to express. Usually such an expression cannot be recalled, and perhaps it might be hard to forget or to forgive. It is one thing to have serious differences of opinion when in control of all your faculties but quite another to shoot off your mouth while your brain is under the influence of a stimulant.

2. Don't quarrel late at night. It's not too easy to think straight when you are tired. The argument might better be held in abeyance until you can exercise some logic.

3. Don't overdo those quarrels. There is no use making so much of a good thing that it loses its appeal. One argument several hours after another leads to more than even the strongest personality can handle. Have a breathing space so as to recoup your senses.

4. Don't argue in a car. I've been a passenger in the back seat of a car in which a hot man-and-wife difference of opinion developed in the front seat. Those are agonizing moments for everyone. Speed picks up, attention is drawn away from the road, red lights become a challenge to be met, and the lives of other innocent drivers may be endangered. The automobile, whether moving or standing still, is a terrible battleground.

5. Don't argue when there are guns within reach. Every day newspapers recount instances when, in a fit of anger, an individual has lost control of himself, and injury or death has resulted.

[2] Rebecca Liswood, *First Aid for the Happy Marriage* (New York: Trident Press, 1965), p. 180.

GUIDELINES TO A HEALTHY QUARREL

In observing the disintegration of a marriage in middle age, one can look back on the earlier years and see what kind of games have been played. The quarrels have shifted from the cause of the problems to the way the quarrels are carried on. There are guidelines that counselors have drawn up so that the couple drifting apart can reorient themselves. Honest reevaluation is not always easy at this time, but it is necessary if quarrels are indeed to prove constructive.[3]

1. Express opinions, desires and concerns in as calm and lucid a way as possible. Be willing to listen as well as talk.

2. In the heat of an argument, the point of view of another person seems to make little sense. One of the virtues needed here is an appreciation of how the other person feels or thinks.

3. Timing is a most important factor in a dispute. After being confined all day at home, many women are all too ready to let loose their pent-up feelings. However, when he first enters the house may not be a good time for the wife to tell the husband about his failure to fix the leaky faucet. Nor is he likely to respond favorably to the news of a neighbor's kid tearing off her prize flowers and a request to "do something about it."

Nor is this the moment for the husband to vent his own frustrations of the day on his wife. Just because he has had a bad day is no reason to find fault with her housekeeping or her neglect of a chore he had "assigned" to her. Mealtime and bedtime are not good quarrel times. "Right now" is not necessarily right. The matter must be brought into the open but there's no point in ruining a good meal or a good night's sleep.

4. Referring to one's wife as a "bitch" or one's husband as a "stubborn jackass" serves no effective purpose. Name-calling should be avoided.

---

[3] Norman M. Lobsenz and Clark W. Blackburn, *How to Stay Married* (New York: Cowles Publishing Co., 1968), p. 103.

5. Change your tune. Too many husbands and wives overwork such expressions as "you never do anything right," "you're cuckoo," or "if that isn't just like a man (woman)."

6. Avoid particularly vulnerable areas of weakness. Some men cannot drive a nail without bending it. It is of no value to consistently harp on his inability to fix anything. Some women have no talent for cooking or sewing. To wound simply for the sake of hurting is bound to lead to unhappiness. What husband or wife wants to be reminded of shortcomings he is only too aware he possesses?

7. After many years of married life, there are bound to be a few subjects amply covered by previous arguments. It is even worse if these subjects are not relevant to the point at hand. Old scores are best left behind, for they offer no aid in solving the current problem. There is no point in telling your wife of twenty years that she should squeeze the toothpaste tube from the bottom and not from the top when you are commenting on her failure to have supper ready at the appointed time.

8. We have already referred to the danger of silence in a "discussion" situation, allowing misunderstanding to fester like a growing boil. Find a time to hash it out.

9. Some authorities recommend the use of restrained violence—nothing so vigorous as to later require dental appointments or stitches. One psychiatrist said that a *soft* blow delivered by the husband to his wife after she becomes too flirtatious at a party at least shows he cares for her. The only problem is that even restrained violence can get out of hand. Usually the woman comes out on the short end of a physical fight. Women have been known to retaliate by biting, scratching, kicking, or throwing things with an amazing degree of accuracy. Some husbands unhappily discover that their wives have been secretly taking judo lessons.

10. Noise is no substitute for reason. Shouting at each other when you are three feet apart only causes the deci-

bels to rise. Exorbitant threats of divorce, suicide, or name-calling get nowhere. "Let's be calm about this" is a better tack.

11. Some quarrels simply cannot be resolved. On occasion, nations have discovered there does not need to be a winner and a loser. The game can end in a tie and be left at that or played off at a later date. So in an argument, it might be expedient to call a truce. It is proper to conclude that a solution cannot be found and let it go at that. In the future, it may be best simply not to argue about the same thing again.

12. What about tears? Who can say? At the proper moment tears may produce compassion. On the other hand, the husband might find them only a source of annoyance. He succumbs at the moment but, having been pushed into a corner, may reopen the battle later.

THE END OF THE ARGUMENT

How does one end a quarrel? The positive way is to try to reach a solution, perhaps one not considered possible before. Another way is for the man or wife to accept the other's viewpoint. While this is amicable on the surface, the danger is that the acquiescent partner may harbor deep-seated resentments which surface in other ways.

While an apology or apologies might seem in order, too many times this can be a demeaning tactic. It is better to end the argument with an expression of fondness or a reassurance that no permanent damage has been done to the relationship.

The finest conclusion of an argument is to feel that no matter how troublesome the problem or discussion has been, it is still better that way than being separated.

7 SEX IS BEAUTIFUL —AND ENJOYABLE

The praying mantis is one of the most misunderstood insects in the world. We think that when it prays it is saintly, but instead what happens in a praying mantis family could make the devil jump with glee. As the insects copulate, the female bites off the head of the male, and his last gasps of breath combine with his sexual excitement. Once inseminated, the female turns from her sexual interest and eats the male to store up food for her young. This is an unviolated rule of behavior among praying mantises. I am in no way suggesting that man and woman should be as cannibalistic as the mantis but in marriage and sex there are certain facts which, if known, can help a couple achieve, and maintain, a meaningful marriage.

Many of us are still bound by the old-fashioned concepts regarding the discussion of sex. On numerous occasions I have picked up the newspaper to read that parents are heated up because sex is being taught in the public schools. Then there is the minister who objected to pictures of the statue of David, adorned only by a fig leaf, being incorporated into a church school book. He carefully tore them all out. These individuals are reminiscent of persons who used to hide in the basement to look at the *National Geographic* magazine to see if there were pictures of topless natives in far away places or who used to giggle secretly at certain passages of *Gone with the Wind.* Such people regard the teaching and discussing of sex in public places as "something most of us do not talk about."

In our enlightened age there will be those who honestly and sincerely believe that a publishing house which has a religious heritage should not be involved in publishing books on sex and marriage. As one pious clergyman said to me, "People can read that in secular publications and go down to Times Square and see all they want."

Many of us in middle age are upset, whether outwardly or subconsciously, over the present-day concepts of sex. We secretly may enjoy seeing pictures of nudes and X-rated films and reading "juicy" material in books and magazines, but we are not uninhibited to the point where we can discuss sex openly and constructively with our families or in serious conversation in groups.

This is not alarming. Even some doctors appear embarrassed by questions regarding sex. As a matter of fact, at the University of Amsterdam a professor, Conrad Boas, has been hired to teach love. Dr. Boas teaches medical students the art of treating patients who suffer from frigidity, sexual embarrassment, impotence, and other related illnesses which contribute to incompatibility. The reason for the course is that nine out of ten physicians are considered to be hopelessly inadequate to deal with sexual complaints. In the United States it has been held in many medical circles that the average practitioner knows little more about sex than his patients.

That up-tight feeling, the shyness that results when the subject is brought up, needs to be relaxed. Sex should be an enjoyable relationship in the life of a middle-age couple, a grand and glorious dimension of married life. If we acquire a healthy, uncomplicated feeling about sex, we can take a first step toward a better marriage.

Sex is neither dirty nor degrading. A man and woman should derive pleasure from the sex act. Victorian prudery is out of date in our decade. However, let's watch out for a new kind of modern Victorianism. Deane W. Ferm, a lecturer at Mount Holyoke College, says,

> The old Victorians were wrong in their debasement of sex as the new Victorians are in the cheapening of sex. It is ironic that both the old and the new Victorians have tried to sepa-

rate sex and love, the former equating sex with illicit affairs outside of marriage, thereby vulgarizing it, and the latter profaning it as the natural outcome of any meaningful relationship.[1]

He goes on to say that sex and love should not be separated because love embraces sex. Sex does not cause love; it's the other way around.

Sex is fun. The sex act is a physical culmination of a warm marital relationship, not merely biological lust. There is tenderness, "I love you"; trust, "I, Joel, take thee, Donna"; permanence, "in plenty and in want, in joy and in sorrow, in sickness and in health." A deep awareness of one another is an ingredient that makes for a healthy sex life by middle age. Out of a striving for human understanding will come intimate affection and love for each other.

MORE THAN AUTOMATED MACHINES

From what we might gather in the spoken, written and viewed work, our primary concern these days is sex in the biological sense. A full page ad in *The New York Times Book Review* is headed "Rocketing up the best seller lists —150,000 copies in print and 50,000 more on the way." This would make any competing publisher jealous and a writer whose "great" book has never sold more than 5,000 copies envious. David Reuben's new book *Any Woman Can*, the story of love and sexual fulfillment, is just one of a whole new bag that is full of advice that promises ecstasy and approval.

Drs. William Masters and Virginia Johnson measure orgasmic function in their St. Louis clinic as if we were automated machines whose primary purpose is to make sex a performing art. Publications on the necessity for perfecting the proper techniques in sex deal quite explicitly

---

[1] Deane W. Ferm, *Responsible Sexuality—Now* (New York: Seabury Press, 1971), p. 134.

with four-letter words, omitting one—love. Most of what is written reflects the opinion that a woman has to deliver an entertaining program or else she is not fulfilling her role.

A woman of forty-five became worried and concerned over this very thing. She had gone to a bridge party with three of her friends and during the course of the conversation, she had come to the conclusion that she had not enjoyed sexual relations through the years as much as the others had. She had lived through twenty years of her marriage with what she had presumed to be a satisfactory sex life. Now she wondered if she was maladjusted, whether she and her husband really "belonged together." Her friends had talked about those things which "everyone is doing these days with sex" and she had doubt sown in her mind on whether or not she was a "full" woman.

With so much emphasis on technique, there is a tendency to consider only the performance; marriage is cheating itself out of love and a day-by-day human relationship. In technique-oriented books such as *The Sensuous Man* and *The Sensuous Woman*, not only is the woman regarded as a kind of personal whore, but the man is regarded as a performing seal. A man who can have half a dozen orgasms a night and keep an erection for half an hour is complimented. The average woman reading such a book is bound to be disappointed when she considers her husband's performance. He, in turn, may feel his wife is letting him down when she does not conform to the description of women in the books.

When a couple is in love, both of them are real persons with a freedom to have personal tastes and choices. Unfortunately, a man and wife can be all too vulnerable because they seriously want to love and be loved. If they depend on complicated techniques then they are liable to be disappointed to learn that there is more needed than the promise that "all you have to do is. . . ." Eventually they may echo the words of the rather cynical contemporary song, "Is that all there is?"

In my profession, I have taken many photographs and have learned that it is most important to have the proper focus before pushing the shutter button. In middle age, our focus ought to be on love. It is an action word, vital and invigorating. Hard to define precisely, love is described as "the total involvement with any other individual, with his uniqueness as well as his common humanity."

Sex can best be appreciated in the context of a love relationship. In such a framework, you are not going to have a woman going to bed in a diaphanous black nightgown simply to "turn on " a man for physical satisfaction. Neither is he going to exploit and coerce the woman with "But you've never tried it. . . . Everybody does it. . . . Don't be so inhibited. . . . Don't be such a cold fish." These are approaches that can destroy a love relationship.

Both parties must be willing to be involved in love—this deepest expression and fulfillment of a personal encounter. Love includes tenderness, compassion, fidelity, and trust. It is the framework on which sex will work so that it does not merely become a "one-night stand."

We might conclude that by the time we have reached middle age, love would have run its course. Wrong! It is at this stage in life that love begins to grow and be enriched. The sex act becomes more than a mere jumping in and out of bed; it is the significant dimension of the deeper covenant.

In middle age, affection and companionship are as important as the sex act. Couples in the empty-nest period have a good marriage when it is based on love. They have discovered that sexual needs can be greatly satisfied with a highly developed love component whether or not it culminates in sexual intercourse. Theirs is a perpetual courtship that was begun during the youthful days of courtship and has gone into the wedding and right through to middle age. I have watched couples as they have grown older together and have noted their need for closeness, affection, and intimacy that still centers on romance.

"THERE'S SNOW ON THE ROOF, BUT THE FIRE STILL BURNS"

Love is the primary force, and sex is a pleasurable by-product that does not need to be discarded at the age of fifty. While realizing that marriage needs love, we must also consider some changes that take place gradually in middle age, affecting our sexual life.

Not much scientific research has been available regarding the sex life in middle age and later because so many investigators are hamstrung by their own attitudes which they tend to carry into the studies. There are unexpressed taboos about older men and women which hinder completely accurate research. However, Masters and Johnson did make a laboratory study of post-menopausal women and older men and noted some important physiological changes that take place. Their major conclusions are unequivocal: "There is no time limit drawn by the advancing years to female sexuality" and under the proper physical and emotional conditions for the male there is "a capacity for sexual performance that frequently may extend to and beyond the eighty-year-old level." [2]

In the thirty-nine older men studied, Masters and Johnson found evidence that physical sexual response weakened with age. Erection took longer, ejaculation lacked force and duration and sex flush was markedly reduced; greater time was required before another erection could be reached, and so on. They added that there was reason to believe that when sexual expression was maintained

---

[2] From *Sexuality and Man*, Study Guide No. 12 "Sexual Life in the Later Years" by Isadore Rubin (New York: Charles Scribner's Sons). Copies of this pamphlet can be ordered from Sex Information and Education Council, 1855 Broadway, New York, N.Y. 10023.

regularly and the health of the couple remained good, a sexually stimulative climate in the marriage could be achieved.[3]

> Kinsey investigators had reported little evidence of any aging in the sexual capacities of women and had noted that over the years most females had become less inhibited. In contrast to younger women, many of whom did not wish to have intercourse as often as their husbands did, women in later years of marriage expressed the desire to have intercourse more often than their husbands,

said Isadore Rubin, editor of *Sexology Magazine* and author of *Sexual Life After Sixty.*

At Duke University Center for the Study of Aging and Human Development, it was found that as men became older their sexual interest and activity showed a rise, although the physical sexual response might weaken.

When I attended the White House Conference on the Aging, I interviewed Justus "J.D." Stevens, who is ninety-five years old and "having the time of his life." Five times a widower, he was planning to marry again on his return to Salt Lake City. "I'll get me a housekeeper if I possibly can. It's too lonesome to be alone." When most men have lost their verve and vitality, provided they have lived that long, Mr. Stevens was honest when he said, "I love my women." He shyly admitted that the knot was as good as tied with a seventy-nine-year-old widow. J.D. is one person who proves that even though age does reduce the urge for sexual response, there is no automatic cut-off point for sexual interest, desire, or ability.

There have been all kinds of studies made of the physical changes of women in middle life. Peter T. Chew, writing in *The National Observer,* describes the middle-age female as noting "a slight creping of the neck, a faint

---

[3] For a complete treatment of this subject see William H. Masters and Virginia E. Johnson, *Human Sexual Response,* Section IV, "Geriatric Sexual Response" (Boston: Little, Brown & Co., 1966).

tapioca-jiggle of the upper thighs, and crow's feet at the temples. Jane's curvy 120 pounds have started to redistribute themselves into a more rounded form. And insult of insults in a land of breast worshippers: a touch of mammary sag."

Menopause involves the cessation of menstruation and the end of a woman's reproductive capacity. Reactions differ. It bothers some, while others shout "Hallelujah!" because they no longer suffer nervousness, insomnia, hot flashes, loss of vitality and other assorted aches and pains once the menopausal period is over. More than anything else, they feel free from the worry of bearing any more children. These women, rather than bogging down over the concern regarding loss of femininity, become relaxed so that they can enjoy their married life to a greater degree.

Not as much is known about physical and emotional changes in mid-life for men. The so-called masculine climacteric or "change of life" is a mysterious and neglected area of scientific research, possibly because men do not want to talk about it to anyone, not even a researcher.

Recently some fresh insights on the topic have come from a team of six psychologists, psychiatrists, and sociologists at Yale University. They have been engaged in a "Social Study of the Male Mid-Life Decade." The project still is in preparation but some preliminary findings indicate that after forty a man begins to have some fundamental doubts about his work, family, and goals he has set for himself. They may not worry him enough to make him take action, but he does notice a change in his body—the pot belly, the "passion rolls" around the waist, baldness, a tired feeling. But the researchers believe that the biological factors, including the decline of sperm production, have only a small role in the change of life. Most of the problem is psycho-social.

Prof. Daniel L. Levinson, a psychologist, says, "We find

that many men have problems of intimacy with their wives around this time. If there's dissatisfaction with the relationship, it is not due to bodily changes but because these men have altered in their emotional life. They still have a large capacity for affection and passion." [4]

This is reassuring to those of us who may have been worried. We are no longer bright young men bursting with promise, but we can at least look youthful with a bright shirt, tie, blazer, and possibly a toupee. We need not lie down and die but can actually have a rebirth so that we can generate new energies and commitments. I like to think of this period as a time when one takes a look at the present and future and reorganizes life around new goals and satisfactions.

I have read in a national magazine where some men have gone so far as to give up their jobs in corporations and take new responsibilities where the demands are not as strenuous or in some cases are merely different. In middle age they have not stayed in a rut but have ventured out into new endeavors, many times at a sacrifice in salary. Thus an accountant becomes a stockboy in a huge department store; a business executive becomes a teacher on a college campus; a man follows an entirely new line of interest, perhaps moving to a different locale.

While men do not change drastically in a physical sense, a "change of life" does occur. It is reflected in the mode of living, views of life, and relations with others.

What can a man do to win the battle of the middle years? Professor Levinson puts it this way:

> Each man must find his own course. He should come to terms with himself and acknowledge that he is in his middle years. He must accept the fact that he can't be as athletic as he used to be and that decline in sexual vigor is common-

[4] Quoted in T. K. Irwin, "The Baffling Changes a Man Goes Through in His Middle Years," *Family Weekly* magazine (Oct. 24, 1971), p. 6. Reprinted by permission.

place and natural. His special task is to continue to develop, to grow up. . . . He must know himself and find himself. That's what it's all about.[5]

PROBLEMS ARE NOT INSURMOUNTABLE

While age alone does not bring on sexual problems, Masters and Johnson's clinical work with older males has led them to describe six general groups of factors which are responsible for much of the loss of sexual responsiveness in later years. These factors need to be considered by both men and women, for in a good marriage, understanding and cooperation are important.

Boredom and monotony. If this is the culprit in your marriage, then a practical lesson is in order. By rigidly adhering to the outworn notion that only certain methods of love-making are right and proper and that others are degrading and perverted, you are placing a limit on your enjoyment of sex.

This does not mean you have to try every new method suggested in *The Sensuous Man* or *The Sensuous Woman.* However, there is nothing wrong with reexamining the conditions under which coitus takes place and the variety of positions for intercourse. Dr. Rubin points out that in middle and later years erection is not easily attained just by cerebral stimuli. In other words, all those girlie pictures in the magazines, to which it has been remarked "young men and clergymen subscribe," begin to look alike by middle years. But, says Dr. Rubin, older men can often achieve a completely satisfactory tactile or reflex erection by penile massage and manipulation with the understanding and cooperation of the wife.

Joseph Wolpe, professor of psychiatry at Temple University Medical School, and Arnold Lazarus, director of the Behavior Therapy Institute in Sausalito, California, suggest that anxiety in coital performance can be lessened if the male knows there are several ways besides direct

[5] Ibid., p. 7.

genital contact by which his partner can obtain full satisfaction. "Proficiency in these (oral, manual, and digital) manipulations," they say, "provides powerful sources of sexual arousal."

Worth repeating is the necessity for both men and women to maintain attractiveness and sex appeal to the fullest extent possible. Eileen Ford, whose Ford Model Agency provides coveys of beautiful women for the fashion industry, gives a clue on why there is boredom in marriage.

> Too many women are dull to their husbands for physical as well as mental reasons. These may sound like old clichés, but they're true. Such women never change their hair style, their lipstick color, their perfume. They don't pay attention to their nightgown. They see him off to the office with rollers in their hair—and that's the memory of her that he will have all day, while those cute little secretaries in miniskirts are something else.[6]

Mrs. Ford feels that most men are "male chauvinist pigs." She does not accept the 50–50 proposition in marriage as workable but believes the woman has the heavier responsibility, unfair as that may be, and must keep herself alluring to keep the marriage going.

Joyce Brothers does have some suggestions for women. She feels that women should not retire from competition and figure that they will be able to hold their companions automatically. Women need to remember that an older man looks better and better to the widow, to the left-over girl who made a career first and is looking for a husband and to the teenage beauty who goes for older men. Dr. Brothers suggests to women that they work harder at being loving wives by turning on the charm. A side effect will be, hopefully, that the husband will make himself more attractive too.

There is a television commercial that shows an alluring

[6] Quoted in Peter T. Chew, "Faithful Old Jane Faces Middle Age and Her Mirror," *The National Observer* (Nov. 27, 1971), p. 16.

middle-age woman who has corralled her man and knows how to hold him. She gazes lovingly into his eyes as he confides to the privacy of the television camera that no matter how busy she is every day, keeping house, getting meals, attending meetings, when day is done she's as lovely as ever because she takes Geritol. "I think I'll keep her," he says adoringly, hugging her close. If this connubial bliss is to survive, one would hope that he will have a better foundation than Geritol on which to base mutual understanding and love.

Preoccupation with career and economic pursuits. In the early years of marriage the husband is busy trying to move up the ladder in his job, to raise a family, to educate his children, to provide a home and to earn enough to pay his taxes. When the kids leave home, one would think that this point might be comparable to reaching the peak of a mountain and being able to calmly look over the valley and enjoy the view. However, it doesn't always seem to work out that way. It's more like Moses climbing Mount Nebo. He got to the top to see the Promised Land but never was privileged to set foot in it.

When we get to middle age we have not reached the Promised Land. We find we have new mountains to conquer, new crises to face. The kids are gone, but now we have a choice of looking forward eagerly or unhappily toward retirement which we suddenly realize is not too far off. The fifties can indeed be difficult years for a couple.

Trying hard to keep up with his work, a man may feel the effects of pressure. He gets tired, slows down. There are slips of memory; he feels vitality dwindling and suddenly realizes the age difference between himself and the younger men at the office. As he desperately tries to strike out in new directions, he sees doors begin to close and possibilities narrow. He learns, to his surprise, that even he is expendable.

Though his job may not be in jeopardy, his ego does

not want to accept the fact that younger men can and are taking over responsibilities that once were his. With these burdensome thoughts, the man may arrive home at night with sex the farthest thing from his mind. So it may be with the working wife. She is so fatigued by the competition in the business world that bed merely suggests sleep.

The quality of our sex life could be improved if in middle age we might consider the advice of Benjamin Spock. He feels that there should be a major revision of our American philosophy and priorities along the lines that so many of our young people advocate:

> A simpler style of living in terms of size and style of our houses; fewer, smaller automobiles (more travel on bicycle and on foot); much less in the way of gadgets and possessions of all kinds; simpler, cheaper clothes (blue jeans for people of all ages); much less striving for money, position and power. Instead, an emphasis on service to fellow men, in the spirit of brotherly love.[7]

Mental and physical fatigue. Since this topic has been alluded to earlier, it is enough to add here that it is a fast world we live in and most of us are too tired for our own good. We do not spend enough time relaxing, a statement which is easy to make but hard to carry out. We do not take the time to show affection.

A middle-age man who worked in a highly competitive office went to his doctor for his regular yearly checkup. Afterward he asked, "Doctor, can you do something for my wife? She's frigid." When the doctor talked to the wife, he heard another story. The husband consistently came home from work tense, irritable, cranky, and demanding. He talked frequently of the tensions he faced on the job, the competition and the dog-eat-dog way in

---

[7] From "What Makes a Happy Family?" by Benjamin Spock, M.D., *Redbook* (November 1971), p. 69. © 1971 by The McCall Publishing Company.

which he had to do business. The tension was reflected in the household. To seek relief from all this, he demanded and expected intercourse every night, giving little thought to his wife's feelings. As a result of his boorishness, she developed headaches, became depressed and soon had a long list of psychosomatic symptoms. She had not gone to the doctor and out of a sense of devotion to her husband, did not complain aloud. But her feelings were inadvertently shown in the bedroom.

Even in the fast-paced world in which we live there should be periods of rests, slowdowns. Leroy "Satchel" Paige offered some sage advice on relaxation:

1. Avoid fried meats which anger up the blood.
2. If your stomach disputes you, lie down and pacify it with cool thoughts.
3. Keep the juices flowing by jangling around gently as you move.
4. Go lightly on the vices—the social ramble ain't restful.
5. Avoid running at all times.
6. Don't look back; something might be gaining on you.

I wouldn't go so far as to guarantee sexual responsiveness if you follow these rules, but I'm positive you will feel more relaxed and contented. Who knows? A better sexual relationship might just be the result.

Overindulgence in food and drink, especially alcoholic beverages. Knowing what we do about the possibility of a sexual slowdown in the fifties and later, why aggravate the situation by becoming obese? The amounts of food we once ate without gaining weight now seem to add those extra pounds. If you fill up with a big dinner, you can be fairly sure your mind will not dwell on sex. You may blame your sexual problem on frigidity or impotence but actually find that the difficulty is your stomach and liver.

This ties in with alcoholic consumption. There is no point in going into a long dissertation on the misuse of alcohol; this in itself would be another book. Most social drinkers and alcoholics don't want to hear about their problem anyway. But if you are having sexual problems and use liquor with any frequency, this may be one reason for your trouble. Although it's long been held that excessive drinking damages the brain, a new report contends that even moderate social drinking destroys brain cells.

According to Melvin H. Knisely, professor of medical anatomy at the Medical College of South Carolina, even a little alcohol is not little enough. In his report to the Twenty-eighth International Congress on Alcohol and Alcoholism, he offered to show that when a drinker begins to feel giddy, a few of his brain cells are being killed. In an extension of this, a heavy drinking bout can destroy or damage as many as ten thousand such cells.

Physical aspects. Sometimes physical problems do contribute to the dwindling of sexual response. Unfortunately, there are myths and misconceptions about the body which, if not cleared up, make for difficulties where none need exist.

Somewhere along the line someone, no doubt a man who hated women, started the rumor that through coitus a man could burn himself out by middle age. All I can say is, "What a way to go!" As a matter of fact, the contrary is true. As mentioned before, regularity of sexual expression in the years up to the age of fifty would help to continue sexual activity after that milestone is passed.

Another myth is that intercourse and the emission of semen tends to hasten old age and death. A doctor, asked about this, laughed and said that the emission of semen isn't any more serious than the loss of saliva.

In cases where there is some type of heart problem, especially in the case of the man, it would be well for him to consult his physician regarding intercourse. Fear has been instilled in some men because they have read that men die of heart attacks while having sexual relations. Concern over this has prevented husbands from enjoying sex when in reality there was no basis for fear. Naturally, the heart beats more rapidly and the blood pressure goes up, but if you have no history of cardiac problems, why worry? If you do have problems, talk to your doctor and follow his advice.

A hysterectomy is considered by some women and even a few of their husbands as an automatic end to a couple's sex life. This is not true. Nor does the removal of the prostate gland in men preclude sex. It has been found that sexual response can be carried on to the same degree as prior to surgery. There may be some emotional disturbances because of a fear of the loss of femininity or masculinity but these can be overcome through therapy and the reassurance of the doctor. Most helpful is the understanding, consideration, and encouragement of the mate during the time of distress and uncertainty.

With the emphasis on health and organic foods, some individuals think that vitamins, herbs, and spices will get the juices flowing again in the middle years. Some of the results are by the power of suggestion. Of course, if you are eating a slice of organic bread and a shapely girl goes by, you may give credit to the bread. The Kinsey investigators noted, "Good health, sufficient exercise and plenty of sleep are still the most effective aphrodisiacs known to man."

Fear of unsatisfactory performance. Masters and Johnson feel that many males have a tendency to withdraw from sexual activity rather than to go through any kind of ego-shattering experiences that relate to sexual inadequacy. It is at this point when males panic and turn to extra-marital affairs to "prove" their virility and masculinity.

Sometimes sexual intercourse can be omitted altogether. At a therapy clinic on Long Island the new program provides that a couple be instructed not to engage in intercourse for a time but to enjoy simple body-to-body contact and mutual explorations and expressions of affection. A fear of failure is ruled out over a "successful performance." As a result, there is less sexual stress, improved husband and wife relations and other benefits.

TOO MUCH OR NOT ENOUGH?

This matter of sex obviously does not end here. I've tried to touch on a few aspects of it as it applies to middle age, but actually volumes could be written on the subject and it still would not be complete. One thing is certain; we cannot hide our heads and ignore sex. It's been here for a long time and the way things look now, it will be here quite a while longer.

Under the headline "Man's Relentless Drive," the *Chicago Daily News* published a scientific article that read in part:

> Men up to age 35 have a sexual thought an average of every ten minutes; from age 35 to 50, every 25 minutes; and from 50 on, once an hour. Dr. Joseph B. Trainer, professor of medicine at the University of Oregon, cited these figures, compiled by other researchers, to support his thesis that man, unlike other animals, is impelled toward sex almost continually.

I am not sure how anyone could be "bugged" to see how often he thinks about sex. I could, under some circumstances, think of sex more frequently than every hour. And the reverse is true. Up in the north woods while hunting deer, I wouldn't be inclined to think of sex for some time.

Nevertheless sex is here. Perhaps we have put too much emphasis on sex. That is what was learned in Germany. At one time, advertising companies competed with one another to create the most highly sexed sales pitch for everything from cosmetics to furniture.

Now they are coming to the reluctant admission that sexual oversell may be killing sales. In his book *Selling with Sex*, Jorg Himmermehr says, "Sex in advertising is like a germ with a shorter and shorter incubation period." It has been learned that women are immune to sex oversell, and often reject it outright. According to Dr. Michaelz Ridling of the Institute for Motivation Research in Munich, "the closer you get to the bed, the stronger the rejection by women."

This applies to men as well. When a large drug company decided to market their product "Mister L," they noticed that when they changed from a "sexy" sales approach to one of romantic appeal, it doubled its share of the German cosmetic market.

Few people can agree on just how much sex is enough and how much is too much. Maybe it all depends on the person to whom you are talking. Most men give high priority to sexual intercourse with women to whom they are emotionally attached. Most women, on the other hand, rank companionship, a home, security, love, and affection higher than sex. It would be best for us to keep both these attitudes in mind in the period after the kids leave home. Understanding is the main ingredient to continuing a good marriage.

A GAME TO PLAY

Make a written list of sexual acts which you think would please your partner, limiting the number to ten. Make a list of sexual acts which would please *you* most. Have your husband or wife do the same. Sit, facing each other, and discuss the lists.

Now . . . go to bed. Enjoy yourself!

8 KEEP THE JOYOUS OUTLOOK

In a Blondie and Dagwood comic strip, Dagwood listens as his boss, Mr. Dithers, says, "Cora and I have quarreled since the day we were married."

Sympathetically, Dagwood asks, "You mean you didn't even enjoy the honeymoon?"

"Oh, yeah," responds Mr. Dithers, "the honeymoon was wonderful! They had a bowling alley right in the hotel."

Doctors have said that cheerful people resist disease better than glum ones. One doctor, in fact, tells his patients that the "surly" bird catches the worms.

Despite the overwhelming evidence in favor of maintaining a sense of humor in these times, however, we find just the opposite happening. The current youth culture, theater, and popular fiction present so many of our activities as joyless business, the enemy of laughter, oppressive to free and open spirits with a comic flair. As has been pointed out in an indictment of the church, the clergy and the undertaker both wear black suits.

Our contemporary world tends to be too solemn and serious in its outlook. We find we are unable to laugh at ourselves, at our hopes and at our fears. Some psychiatrists and medics see the growing intensity of the drug scene—along with alcoholism, frenetic activity and other forms of escape—as a by-product of our lost sense of humor. If Freud was correct in stating that laughter is the opening valve to release anxiety, then the world certainly needs to be laughing more today than at any other time in its history. The ridiculous ways in which men and women behave, from those in lowly positions to those at the highest levels of leadership, offer us plenty of "resource material."

Jonathan Miller has diagnosed a disease called "cataplexy" as an acute need to laugh coupled with the incapacity to do so. The diagnosis seems applicable to our times; we need to cultivate the ability to laugh.[1]

One of the places in which humor has an essential place is marriage. Marriages that are under pressure, where problems such as denigrating the other partner or showing a lack of appreciation or interest or presenting a façade for the outside world, can be helped by the partners retaining, or in some cases gaining, a sense of humor. I am not thinking here of humor that seeks to reduce anxiety by merely providing an escape from reality nor a humor that tries to laugh everything away. What is needed is what has been described as "hard-won maturity of delight."

The late Reinhold Niebuhr, a distinguished theologian, said in effect that faith and laughter deal with the incongruities of life. This sort of humor is possible because it is allied with God "who sits in the heavens and laughs." A couple must be able to laugh at themselves or eventually they will take themselves too seriously.

Editors of magazines, books, and newspapers have found that marriage is always a good subject for a cartoon or comic strip. Nightclub and television comedians constantly "take off" on some aspect of marriage. The interesting thing is that the situations described have elements of truth in them. The popular television program *All in the Family* is funny because in the middle-age couple we see our own foibles and prejudices. Marriage humor is popular, perhaps, because it not only helps us forget ourselves and our troubles for the moment but also shows us we are not alone in our idiosyncracies.

In a Lorain, Ohio, hospital where I had taken my father I

---

[1] David L. Luecke, "Let's Teach People to Laugh Again," *Interaction* (January 1971), p. 20.

found a bulletin board in the center of the waiting room. On both sides were cartoons about dentists and doctors as well as about common problems of the day. One showed a middle-age man saying to his wife, "Here I am in all of this sexual revolution and what has happened? I've run out of ammunition."

In our church in Blue Island, Illinois, we used to have a "smile board" on which people would tack up all kinds of quips and cartoons. I found this one of the most popular spots in the church. Even hardened "gloom" members could be seen occasionally cracking a smile, even if only a small one, as they walked away.

In her book *A Man Called Peter*, Catherine Marshall revealed that her husband's success was due, among other precious gifts, to his concept of life as fun. He found joy in the things he did because of his sense of humor and supply of ready wit. He wrote, "If God for you does not smile, there is something wrong with your idea of God."

It may not seem so from some church worship services I have observed, but it is truly biblical to laugh. In Psalm 2 the writer says, "He that sitteth in the heavens shall laugh." And God must indeed laugh when he sees us taking ourselves so seriously, a welcome relief when we have given him so many things to be sad about.

Christianity is finding out in its celebrations that it is not a religion of long faces; it is a life of joy and laughter. Good clean fun lies dormant and lifeless, however, until we are willing to express it. A marriage that makes humor a part of its daily life finds that the whole world bursts out in music.

WHAT IS HUMOR?

Humor is a well-accepted and effective tool for exposing hypocrisy, deceptive inconsistencies, and the inhumanity of men and society.[2] The dictionary tells us that it "is neither darting nor occasional, for it is more a turn of one's

[2] Ibid., p. 22.

nature, a specific tendency of the disposition . . . humor is sympathetic . . . kindly; its mirth is of a generous, human sort." Unfortunately, too many individuals think of *Playboy* humor, associated with dirty stories or the ridicule of another person, his race, his ideals, his personality. Such humor is not helpful, producing bitterness and cynicism and a generally critical attitude on the part of the person indulging in it.

Like Pat and Mike, humor and laughter are inseparable. Josh Billings has defined laughter as "the sensation of feeling good all over, and showing it principally in one spot." In a tense marriage situation the appreciation of the funny side of life can be an antidote for those problem situations. For example, an impecunious minister protested his wife's purchase of a new dress. Reminded of an earlier promise to economize, she replied, "I guess it was the devil that tempted me." "Then why didn't you say, 'Get thee behind me, Satan?' " "I did," came the answer. "But then he whispered over my shoulder, 'It fits you just beautifully in back, too.' "

Marshall McLuhan, who has been among those who have a sharp perspective of events, points to humor as a most useful purveyor of counterculture, that is, the force most able to move society to a new self-image and direction. If he is right, a couple will find humor a useful probe into their thinking and attitudes. At the same time they can hold humor up as a mirror by which they can see themselves from a new viewpoint.[3]

Certainly our days are serious, harried, hurried, and hectic, and life seems hard, metallic, and overly competitive. What can we do but take time to laugh?

The story goes that a man in his middle years was having all kinds of problems with his marriage, but at one point he felt he was on the verge of solving them all. What sent him into a deep, blue funk was the headlines in the paper—drugs, gangs, police corruption, brutality, jus-

---

[3] Ibid.

tice (or rather, the lack of it), law and order, and a host of other depressing items. So he decided to end it all. He climbed up to the top of the George Washington Bridge and was about to jump into the Hudson River when a policeman saw him. The man of the law climbed up to talk to the depressed citizen. The officer got close enough to reason with the man. The intended suicide responded to his earnest endeavors with, "Look at all the bad news in *The New York Times.*" He handed his copy to the policeman. Then they both jumped.

Rollo May, the psychiatrist, said, "A man with a sense of humor has a way of standing off and looking at problems with a perspective. Anxiety and fear have not gotten him down as long as he can laugh. He possesses the qualities of an essential human being."

Most of us do attempt to make our marriages successful. Sometimes we find ourselves in a mold that is uncomfortable. We pretend and make believe. We are "uptight." When we find a new perspective, we discover a release that makes us free, not afflicted with the perfectionist complex but instead experiencing an inner gaity which, while it may not solve the problem at hand, at least gives a breathing space to marshall new strength.

Unfortunately, not every disposition has an abundance of joy in it or the ability to find humor in difficult situations, at least not at first. Such a person may have to work at it; he may be compelled, like the car rental agency, to try harder than others to achieve a sense of humor.

The book of Proverbs says, "A cheerful heart is good medicine, but a downcast spirit dries up the bones." To paraphrase, a cheerful heart is good medicine, but there is nothing that dries up a marriage more quickly than two gloomy people, or even one gloomy person. And in middle age this is definitely a problem. When the kids were at home, there was someone to kid with, joke about, and tease. At the worst, we were too busy to notice the lack of humor. When the empty-nest period arrived, faults and problems seemed etched more clearly. As the cartoonist has so ably caught it in his sketch of a man and woman looking out the window of their home, the man says, "Well, Doris, the children are grown and gone and now it's just you versus me."

DEVELOPING A SENSE OF HUMOR

If you wanted to become a journalist, what would you do? You would sharpen up your English, study, read, write, and observe. The process might involve going to the library, to classes during the day or at night; it certainly would involve practice in writing. You would train yourself by *doing*. If you are serious about developing and maintaining a sense of humor, you must follow some simple rules. Like any goal, you must work toward it.

1. Listen to humor. Recorded comedy can be useful in stimulating a humorous attitude. Skits by Mike Nichols and Elaine May rip the surface of routine relationships and invite discussion on what lies below. Bill Cosby and Bob Newhart are other possibilities.

2. Read humor and learn to appreciate it. You will find books, articles, and all sorts of other material on and by humorists. Read the books of America's great humorists such as Mark Twain, Will Rogers, Robert Benchley, or Fred Allen. Ask yourself what qualities they had that made them so popular with audiences and readers throughout the world that they still are quoted today. Look at some contemporary writers such as P. G. Wodehouse, Stephen Leacock, Corey Ford, and Art Buchwald. Try to fit yourself into situations as the authors saw them. Let yourself go—don't be afraid to laugh aloud. A witty book on marriage, such as *Love and Marriage and Trading Stamps* by L. Richard Lessor is a humorous and practical approach to marriage.

3. Approach humor by seeing. The old cliché that one picture is worth a thousand words is still quite true. Some people enjoy looking more than reading. Our magazine used to have a copyeditor who told me that she rarely read *The New Yorker* but purchased the magazine every

month because she enjoyed the cartoons. In doctors' offices we find books devoted entirely to cartoons, possibly to get the patients' minds off more serious and painful subjects. Some appreciate television programs such as the Dick Van Dyke and Mary Tyler Moore shows because these programs momentarily alleviate problems and provide a hearty laugh. Personally, I feel that way about *Laugh-In.* I have to concentrate so intensely to catch everything that I forget my problems. Not all of us are going to enjoy the same thing. You might like a humorous stage play or a film. You may want to watch the masters of comedy—Jonathan Winters, Jack Benny, Art Carney, Sid Caesar, Flip Wilson, Carol Burnett, Phyllis Diller—and you will find humor to suit your taste.

4. Learn to appreciate humor by practice. Remember the story about the guy who decided to take swimming lessons by correspondence? He studied each lesson very carefully and passed all the written tests. He knew the meaning of the backstroke, the breast stroke, the butterfly stroke. However, when the big day came, he leaped into the deep end of the pool and drowned. Why? He had not combined study with actual practice. So it is with developing a sense of humor. Some have more aptitude in this line than others; some will have to practice more assiduously. But it can be done with practice.

At an appropriate moment, tell your wife or husband a story. You may not succeed the first time in causing so much as a ripple; actually the telling may be funnier than the story itself, especially if you forget the punch line. Don't get discouraged. Try again. As your ability to convey humor improves, so will your humorous outlook on events and even the serious current events of the day can have a tinge of humor in them.

OUTLOOK IS ALL-IMPORTANT

Don't take yourself too seriously. Moments of seriousness do have their place. We can't be laughing baboons all of the time. However, it is easy to take oneself too seriously.

Most of us have difficulty laughing at ourselves, at our hopes and fears, at our future and past and at our successes and failures. When those difficult situations in our marriage arise, as they are bound to, we are prone to let them master us unless we can take the lighter look. Purposely look for the wry side to the situation.

Carol Burnett, the popular television comedienne, says that she stays cheerful by *accenting the bright side.* "Maybe I'm an idiot, but I look in the mirror every morning and say, 'Hi, beautiful!' Even the rain cheers me up; it's so dreary, it makes me feel good by comparison." Some situations may take a lot of looking at before it's possible to find that bright side. It is like the middle-age husband telling his haggard-looking wife, "You've got a stove, a refrigerator, a washing machine, an electric roaster, and a dishwasher. The trouble with you is you don't know how to be happy."

Let humor and light conversation work for you. When I was in the pastoral ministry in Alliance, Ohio, my ministerial colleagues and I, after dropping our church announcements at the *Alliance Review,* would find it relaxing to sit and talk for half an hour over a cup of coffee at a corner restaurant. The conversation had absolutely nothing to do with church work. As a matter of fact, it was definitely on the light and frivolous side, but this is what made it relaxing. Similarly, small talk is important at home as well. It is not always necessary to be wrapped up in deep conversations about money, sex, the job, or the state of national or local political affairs, important as these may be.

Marriage really is fun. Many of us get upset over something that happens during the day, worrying over what might happen next. Middle age, as we have said in other chapters, seems to be a time of worry. It's worth a try to get our attention away from ourselves through a laugh prescription instead of a medical one. Free as the polluted air we breathe, learning to smile is good health, a tonic for a sour marriage. A laugh-a-day program for your marriage may sound artificial at first, but as the days pass, you will begin to notice a change. Cultivate that ability to laugh.

Maintain your joy when the going gets rough. A couple celebrating their golden wedding anniversary were asked how they had lived happily together for so long. The husband explained, "We agreed that if we quarreled, my wife was to go to her room until her anger passed, and I was to go outside until she called me back in." "How did it work out?" he was asked. "You can see what fifty years of outdoor living has done for me," came the quick response.

Pick out the cheerful and humorous events that occurred during your rough day and concentrate on them, even if you must search especially hard. If you are tense before you leave work or before your husband is due to arrive home, don't reach for a shot of whiskey to enliven you. Instead, pick up a magazine or book that has some humorous anecdotes or cartoons in it and look them over. Have handy a book that contains a collection of humorous stories. Consider the anecdotes, cartoons, or stories in the light of what is applicable to your particular situation and at an appropriate time be prepared to share them with your husband or wife.

From personal experience, I know that on the way home from work as we ride the commuter train, my friends—John, Martin, Bill—and I sit together. We find that a good story or jovial comment on the events of the day help relieve tenseness that somehow manages to build throughout the day. We usually joke with our conductor, Jack, as well, and he has told me he gets a lift from this joking as much as we do. I am not saying this kind of conversation guarantees making every marriage a bed of ease, but in this topsy-turvy world, it certainly helps.

Coming home from a Chicago trip one day, I felt uptight. Having been on a grueling assignment had taxed my energy, and, at the moment, joy and fun were about as far away as the horizon I could barely see from the airplane window. I realized that such a feeling might not be the best to have when my wife, faithfully waiting at the airport, picked me up.

As we flew along, the stewardess was serving a snack, the usual beef or turkey sandwich. The pilot, intending to switch on the personal intercom to the stewardess must have flipped the wrong switch. At any rate, the message came loud and clear throughout the cabin, "Honey, how about bringing us some snacks up here with a lot of loving?"

The stewardess was flabbergasted and flustered as well. She set down her sandwiches on a seat and made a beeline for the cockpit door. As she headed up the aisle, a voice rang out from one of the passengers, "Hey, honey, you forgot the sandwich!"

That brought a laugh from all of us but more than that, at least for me, it put me in a better frame of mind when I landed at Newark Airport and shared the anecdote with my wife.

You have reason to be joyful. In so many of the articles on marriage that are currently being written, the marriage institution and the world seem to be all gloom and doom. To read some of the articles, one would think if he didn't have some kind of super sex orgies with his mate, passionate love with a mistress or an occasional fling with a stranger that the rest of his life was not worth living. One would do well to follow the challenge of the gospel hymn, even when the days look dark:

> When upon life's billows you are tempest tossed,
> When you are discouraged, thinking all is lost,
> Count your blessings, name them one by one,
> And it will surprise you what the Lord hath done.

And one of the things he has done is to give us a sense of humor. Mark Twain said that man is the only animal that blushes, or needs to. It is also true that man is unique in the sense that he can laugh, and needs to. There is no magic cure-all to our troubles in spite of all the highly advertised panaceas. But if you develop a good sense of humor and keep fun in your marriage, even after the kids leave home, you're going to enjoy it a lot more.

THOUGHTS TO REMEMBER

1. Avoid joking at the wrong time or in the wrong place. If your mate is trying to be serious about something that troubles him or her, wait with that ebullience. Avoid "smart" comments, kidding or jokes at that moment. A word of assurance might be wiser.

2. Don't extend kidding too far. Keep in the spirit of humor, not bitterness.

3. Refuse to take yourself too seriously.

4. Pick out something to laugh about each day and share it.

5. Use humor to knock the knot out of knotty problems.

6. A healthy, faith-full sense of humor keeps us human.

7. Smile, and your mate will smile with you; weep, and you'd better carry your own handkerchief.

TEST YOURSELF

Although there probably is no such thing as a "perfect" marriage, most of us can rate our marriages as satisfactory or unsatisfactory. With the idea in mind that one never does reach the ultimate perfection but rather can continue to work toward that goal, take this brief quiz individually. Then discuss it together as a couple. Hopefully, it will contain suggestions that can help your marriage and will give you a perspective of your life together in the "middle years" when the kids have left home. Be honest in your answers.

Rules for scoring: At the end of each of the following questions you will find a set of five scoring figures—0, 1, 2, 3, 4. On a separate sheet of paper write the figure which represents your answer to each question on this basis:

0 means "never," "not at all."
1 means "somewhat," "sometimes," "rarely," "a little."
2 means "about as often as not," "an average amount."
3 means "usually," "a good deal," "frequently."
4 means "regularly," "practically always," "entirely."

1. Do you face each day with anticipation? .. 0 1 2 3 4
2. Do you concentrate on the future instead of the "do you remember" days? 0 1 2 3 4
3. Do you both sleep in the same room? 0 1 2 3 4
4. Do you embrace spontaneously during the day? 0 1 2 3 4
5. Do you keep up a neat personal appearance and not let yourself go because "no one will see me"? 0 1 2 3 4

6. Do you make a genuine attempt to get away together for a weekend or even a day or evening? 0 1 2 3 4
7. Do you feel truly happy when your spouse receives praise or commendation? 0 1 2 3 4
8. Do you "trust" your spouse with attractive members of your own sex? 0 1 2 3 4
9. Do you tend to be tolerant of your mate's faults rather than emphasize them? 0 1 2 3 4
10. Do you make a conscientious attempt to listen to your spouse when he (she) talks to you? 0 1 2 3 4
11. Do you feel you really understand what your spouse means, not only through conversation but through his (her) actions and reactions as well? 0 1 2 3 4
12. Are you thoughtful in *little* things? 0 1 2 3 4
13. Do you avoid nagging and constant criticism? 0 1 2 3 4
14. Do you discuss your misunderstandings and try to clear them up? 0 1 2 3 4
15. Do you avoid taking yourself too seriously? 0 1 2 3 4
16. Do you make an attempt to look on the bright side of a difficult situation? 0 1 2 3 4
17. Can you handle a crisis effectively? 0 1 2 3 4
18. Do you enjoy your sexual relations with your spouse? 0 1 2 3 4
19. Since the kids have left home, have you felt more uninhibited about expressing your sexual desires? 0 1 2 3 4
20. Now that you are in the "middle years," are you specifically working for your marriage to achieve fulfillment? 0 1 2 3 4

Total your respective scores. A perfect score, of course, would be 80 but this might be difficult to achieve, especially if you are honest. Whatever your score, determine the areas in which you need improvement. Remember, half the battle is won if you both sincerely *desire* to have a rewarding and satisfying relationship, even though the kids have left home and you remain with the "empty nest."

As many couples who have gone through this period of life can attest, these years *can* be the happiest and best of your life.

BIBLIOGRAPHY

Anchell, Melvin. *Sex and Sanity.* New York: Macmillan, 1971.
Bach, G. R. *The Intimate Marriage.* New York: William Morrow & Co., 1969.
Bird, Joseph and Lois. *Marriage Is for Grownups.* Garden City, N.Y.: Doubleday, 1969.
Blood, Robert O., Jr. *Marriage.* New York: Free Press of Glencoe, 1962.
Boyland, Brian Richard. *Infidelity.* Englewood Cliffs, N.J.: Prentice-Hall, 1971.
Burns, R. W. *The Art of Staying Happily Married.* Englewood Cliffs, N.J.: Prentice-Hall, 1963.
Capon, Robert F. *Bed and Board—Plain Talk About Marriage.* New York: Simon and Schuster, 1965.
Carrington, William L. *The Healing of Marriage.* Great Neck, N.Y.: Channel Press, 1961.
Clemens, Alphonse H. *Design for a Successful Marriage.* Englewood Cliffs, N.J.: Prentice-Hall, 1964.
Clinebell, Howard J. and Charlotte H. *The Intimate Marriage.* New York: Harper & Row, 1970.
Dicks, Henry V. *Marital Tensions.* New York: Basic Books, 1967.
Ferm, Deane W. *Responsible Sexuality Now.* New York: Seabury Press, 1971.
Freeman, Lucy and Greenwald, Harold. *Emotional Maturity in Love and Marriage.* New York: Harper & Row, 1961.
Fried, Barbara. *The Middle-Age Crises.* New York: Harper & Row, 1967.
Harrell, Irene. *Good Marriages Grow (A Book for Wives).* Waco, Tex.: Word Books, 1968.
Havard, Alan and Margaret. *Death and Rebirth of a Marriage.* Wheaton, Ill.: Tyndale House, 1970.
Kelly, George A. *The Catholic Marriage Manual.* New York: Random House, 1958.
Landers, Ann. *Truth Is Stranger.* Englewood Cliffs, N.J.: Prentice-Hall, 1968.
Landis, Judson and Mary. *Building a Successful Marriage.* Englewood Cliffs, N.J.: Prentice-Hall, 1963.

Landis, Paul. *Making the Most of Marriage.* New York: Appleton-Century-Crofts, 1960.

Lang, Theo. *The Difference Between a Man and a Woman.* New York: John Day Co., 1971.

Lederer, William and Jackson, Don D. *The Mirages of Marriage.* New York: W. W. Norton & Co., 1968.

Lee, Robert and Casebier, Marjorie. *The Spouse Gap.* Nashville, Tenn.: Abingdon Press, 1971.

Lessor, Richard. *Love and Marriage and Trading Stamps.* Chicago: Argus Communications, 1971.

Liswood, Rebecca. *First Aid for the Happy Marriage.* New York: Trident Press, 1965.

Lobsenz, Norman M. and Blackburn, Clark W. *How to Stay Married.* New York: Cowles Publishing Co., 1968.

Martinson, Floyd M. *Marriage and the American Ideal.* New York: Dodd, Mead & Co., 1960.

Masters, William H. and Johnson, Virginia E. *Human Sexual Response.* Boston: Little, Brown & Co., 1966.

May, Rollo. *Love and Will.* New York: W. W. Norton & Co., 1969.

Menninger, William. *Living in a Troubled World.* Kansas City, Mo.: Hallmark Cards & Co., 1967.

Mouton, Jane Srygley and Blake, Robert R. *The Marriage Grid.* New York: McGraw-Hill, 1971.

Myers, T. Cecil. *Happiness Is Still Home Made.* Waco, Tex.: Word Books, 1969.

Petersen, J. Allan (ed.). *The Marriage Affair.* Wheaton, Ill.: Tyndale House, 1971.

Peterson, J. A. *Married Love in the Middle Years.* New York: Association Press, 1968.

―――――. *Toward a Successful Marriage.* New York: Charles Scribner's Sons, 1960.

Peterson, Mark E. *Guide to a Happy Marriage.* Englewood Cliffs, N.J.: Prentice-Hall, 1964.

Plattner, Paul. *Conflict and Understanding in Marriage.* Richmond, Va.: John Knox Press, 1964.

Purtell, Thelma C. *Generation in the Middle.* New York: Paul Eriksson, Inc., 1963.

Rogers, Carl. *Carl Rogers on Encounter Groups.* New York: Harper & Row, 1970.

Schutz, William C. *Joy, Expanding Human Awareness.* New York: Grove Press, 1967.

Snow, John H. *On Pilgrimage: Marriage in the '70s.* New York: Seabury Press, 1971.

Spotnitz, Hyman and Freeman, Lucy. *The Wandering Husband: Love, Sex and the Married Man.* Englewood Cliffs, N.J.: Prentice-Hall, 1964.

Thielicke, Helmut. *The Ethics of Sex.* New York: Harper & Row, 1964.

Toffler, Alvin. *Future Shock.* New York: Random House, 1971.

Whiston, Lionel. *Are You Fun to Live With?* Waco, Tex.: Word Books, 1968.

Winch, Robert Francis. *Selected Studies in the Family.* New York: Holt, Rinehart & Winston, 1962.

Wood, Leland Foster. *How Love Grows in Marriage.* Great Neck, N.Y.: